G000168120

Praise

Freedom's Way

"*Freedom's Way* has given me both inspiration and practical guidance to help me make the most of my life's journey."

—John Moore, founder and CEO, Advanced Automation, Inc.

"*Freedom's Way* is a breakthrough. It opens your eyes to your untapped potential and reveals new ways of seeing the world."

—Jeff Carter, Professor of Comparative Religion, Author

"I use *Freedom's Way* as a handbook for living. It is not a book to read once. Revisiting is rewarding, necessary."

—Paul Turnock, Social Activist

"The book offers an end to our society's spiritual winter."

—Mis Kamieniak, Film Director

"Rarely will you find a man who can weave an aura with his eloquence both in the written and spoken word."   —The Hindu Times

Freedom's Way

Eternal Principles Aligned to the Realities of Modern Living

Zephyr Bloch - Jorgensen

Freedom's Way

Distributed in The United Kingdom by Gazelle Book Services
Limited White Cross Mills, High Town, Lancaster, LA1 4XS
Tel: 44(0) 152468765 Fax: 44(0) 152463232
Email: Sales@gazellebooks.co.uk

A catalogue record for this book is available from the British Library.

ISBN-13:978-1-920918-01-9 ISBN-10:1-920918-01-9

Cover and internal design by Magnus Andersson, Inner Vision Design, Inc
Photographs: Udaipur at sunrise by Zephyr Bloch-Jorgensen;
back cover photograph by Jane Gold
Typeset in EuropeanExt and BaskervilleTCE fonts by Debra Rivard
Edited by Chris Roerden

Dedicated to my parents and grandmother who set the cornerstone for my life, to my teachers who inspired me to seek, to my friends who helped light my way, to my team who continue to labor to make Freedom's Way a reality for the world, and to you, the reader, who inspired me to write.

Thank you.

Contents

Preface

A BEAUTIFUL ARABIAN tale tells the story of a farmer who lived by the Nile. Every day he used to steer his plow with his beloved ox through a stubborn field. Too often the plow would get caught; always in the same place. This went on for a number of years.

One particularly hot day, the farmer was plowing the field with his ox and his plow caught again in the same place. This day the plow was particularly stuck. The farmer screamed, kicked, and even cursed, but nothing would free it. He collapsed in the shade of his ox, until the sun began to disappear.

The farmer resolved to dig to the point of the plow and to free it. He dug and dug with his hands. By the time the sun was half gone, the farmer realized his plow was caught on something large and metal. He started to dig and brush away the sand around the metal, and soon before him was a golden ring attached to something. The farmer shifted the sand and saw that the ring was attached to a wooden trap door. He gently moved his ox and pulled open the door. Beneath it lay the most beautiful jewels and treasure.

Freedom's Way is my ring. Writing it and living by its principles has changed my life. It took me out of a career in law that stifled my spirit. It gave me the courage to quest inward and brave my fears, and it restored my awe for living.

The two tools in *Freedom's Way* called metacentering and vision drivers have guided me to a bounty of true friends and beautiful relationships filled with energy and honesty. I now hug my father, and he hugs me. My every waking moment is filled with a love of the world and a spontaneous desire to help every person I meet unearth their ring.

It is a great privilege to be able to share *Freedom's Way* with you. I have invested every breath ensuring that your reading experience leads you to your treasure. If you have any questions or simply wish to drop a note, please don't hesitate to email me: zephyr@freedomsway.net.

Zephyr
11 October 2007

May my words and your heart share one way.

Dante Alighieri, *The Divine Comedy*, Paradise, xxxxii

Freedom's Call

What is the Metacenter?

Part 1

New Beginnings

One

THIS IS THE journey of discovering your greater personality and truth — and then living it. It is the greatest adventure you can ever know.

You may think this fantasy; however, if you look into your heart and listen to those who have lived and achieved before us, you'll realize that the greatest resistance to love, freedom, and success is the resistance we place on ourselves. We allow doubt, fears, and insecurities to block us from truth and from our ability to create a better future.

I feel we have lost touch with our hopes and dreams; that we have become strangers to the very forces that gave us life. We dwell on what we could become, and yet, as time passes, we feel little closer to the place we yearn to be. The harder we strive for success, the more it seems to elude us. We have given up on giving life a chance and are trying to brave the storm alone. Yet the more we fight, the more we find ourselves lost.

I believe we have become strangers to the sanctuary within that can lead us to everything we can be and everything we long to become. We have lost touch with this mysterious place that holds the keys to our power. Nevertheless, we are witnessing a resurgence to once again discover this special place within us all.

This mysterious place, this sanctuary of personal power, is echoed through the myths and religions of the ages. No wonder, for it holds a force revered for thousands of years. This force is life's fire, and the joy of feeling this fire is what we have come to know through the ages as love. The fire ignites the love, and the love feeds the fire. One cannot be mastered without the other. Neither can one part exist without the other, as a tree consists of trunk and foliage. The trunk relies on foliage, and the foliage relies on the trunk. The structure gives form to expression, and the expression gives purpose to structure. A deep and intimate relationship between functions has brought the tree into existence. Cultivating our inner sanctuary − our trunk − and allowing it to grow in our daily lives has been a focus of the human journey for millennia.

The expression of our inner sanctuary has been known as love for thousands of years. We call this expression "kindness" and "compassion." To express love rather than hatred, compassion rather than inhumanity, is the bedrock of society.

Our inner sanctuary, however, has eluded labeling, becoming one of the great mysteries. It is elusive because it is invisible to the outside world, escaping our physical senses. The Bhagavad Gita of ancient India speaks of the inner sanctuary in this way:

Weapons do not pierce it,
Fire does not burn it,
Water does not wet it;
Nor does the wind cause it to wither.[1]

Your metacenter

For thousands of years, symbol and word have referred to this inner place. It is described as the "center" or "self," but over time, both have come to mean little. As our inner sanctuary has descended into mystery, so has our relationship to love and power.

Symbols that represent our inner sanctuary include the geometrical shri-yantra, the bi-triangular Star of David, and the cross. All three embody the cataclysmic meeting of opposites — the triumphant joining of heaven with earth, the masculine with the feminine, and the subterranean world of night with the vital world of day.

For the shri-yantra and the Star of David, the center of the symbol is like a temple — potently empty, dynamically still — embodying a force beyond the realm of words.

For the cross, the center is Christ. Like the Buddha, Christ is the ultimate embodiment of what it means to be human, of who we are, and of who we can become.

Although symbol and word encourage us to see the center as fixed and contained, centeredness (as we will explore later) is a continuing, dynamic bringing forth of personal awareness. It is living, not static.

Centeredness is also an unfolding flow into the material plane of the world. It makes the tree whole, where trunk and foliage become one, naturally.

The way we see the center needs to be overhauled. It is more than we have come to know.

Centeredness is a state beyond the ordinary day. It takes us from our material, fixed place of being — where we feel separate from everything and everyone else — to a fresh dimension where we connect with our environment and all living things with whom we share the planet.

This new dimension awakens us to the fact that we are a dynamic event in the unfolding world; and so is everything else around us.

I call this powerful place of being and awakening the *metacenter*. It is a state that unites the severed aspects of our inner world and our outer world. When we are *metacentered*, we remember our vision for life — marriage, family, work, and world — and strive to make that vision reality.

Vision is key. It is a rite of passage. *Metacentering* is the ordeal of breaking free of conforming to the ways of others and seeking out our own lives. In this way, metacentering is the journey to freedom.

Metacentering also brings power. When we shut out our right to power, we shut out our right to be free. The concept of power has its place in all the world's cultures. For instance, people from India call it prana; people from China call it Ch'I; the Melanesians call it Mana; and others call it the Holy Spirit.

Common to all these cultures is the observation that power brings ability and wisdom.

A powerful, metacenterered human being is one who gives and receives love freely and acts in ways aligned with knowledge and strength, not fear and insecurity.

The ever new

As we have lost touch with our inner world and what we are capable of, the expression of the metacenter — love — has gradually decayed. These days, it is flimsy, found more in movies or romance novels than in our day-to-day lives.

Life is crying out for a renewal of love in which we treat one another with dignity and treat ourselves as beings of potential. Love is a force. When we love others, we help them become all they can be. When we love ourselves, we act on wisdom and trust our insight.

To renew love is to return to cherishment. Love never loses contact with wonder; every moment is seen from the eyes of the *ever new.* Love asks us to revere the ordinary: to watch the majesty in a raindrop, the rays of the universe in the eyes of a child — to look *for* instead of look *at.* Love asks us to listen to the symphony of rain against the roof and the windy dance of leaves — to *listen* rather than *hear.* Love asks us to feel the breeze caress our face — to *sense*, not *confront.*

Renewing our reverence for the simple is essential to touch that place within.

We are smothered by a fear that somehow we are alone, cut off from each other. We walk our city's streets with our heads down and eyes fixed to the pavement. We walk as if the only way to live is to obey the norm and follow those who go before us.

Rarely do we ask how things could be improved, or, better still, remade.

This conformist way of living lacks vision. As individuals, we are not tapping the power dormant within us.

Yeats alludes to this in his poem "The Second Coming," which opens:

> *Turning and turning in the widening gyre*
> *The falcon cannot hear the falconer*
> *Things fall apart; the center cannot hold;*
> *Mere anarchy is loosed upon the world,*
> *The blood-dimmed tide is loosed, and everywhere*
> *The ceremony of innocence is drowned;*
> *The best lack all conviction, while the worst*
> *Are full of passionate intensity....*

Our hearts cry out for a return to the *ever new*, pleading with us to resurrect all that is pure, childlike, and magical: to remember glee and wonderment. These qualities help make us whole. When we see with the *ever new,* we live with vitality and drive: difficulty becomes challenge; the daunting and unexpected becomes a call to adventure.

Silent Stillness

Two

THE ROAD TO realizing vision entails risk. When we think about risk, we often picture a radical life change that involves abandoning some element of financial or emotional security, such as leaving a job or a relationship. Risk involves more than a life change, however. Risk requires that we find the courage to change a debilitating belief, to ignore insecurity, and to act with faith.

One of the hardest things human beings can do is face the expectations of their parents, their peer group, and their society, and despite feeling the insistence of these unspoken laws of "correct living," live in a way aligned with their own yearnings and inspirations.

Our history seeps into our lives and taints our present, coloring our attitudes, our beliefs, and even our dreams in insidious ways. As most of us grow older, our self-worth dims, our potential decays, and our faith tires. The health of our attitudes, beliefs, and dreams, so crucial to our success and the experience of life's miracle, weakens. We tend not to see with our own eyes, but with the eyes of the day: what's in, what's out.

Even our definitions of love and success become tainted. Advertising tells us what we need, music tells us what we feel, movies tell us what we aspire to. It takes heroic degrees to let go of your attitudes, beliefs, and dreams — even your image of God — and allow life to show you.

For many, it takes a crisis of mythic proportions to shift a debilitating belief, to strive despite one's past, and to live one's faith. Thankfully, there is an easier way.

Remembering silent stillness

At the heart of your metacenter lies a pristine state of awareness I call *silent stillness*.

The experience of self prior to silent stillness is like standing knee-deep in an angry ocean: the opaque sea breaking on your thighs, the undercurrent pulling your calves. After experiencing silent stillness, the sea is settled; you see your feet on the seabed encircled by the ripples of sand carved by the currents. This can be the experience of your life.

Amidst the stresses of modern living, it is easy to undervalue silent stillness. From the moment we open our eyes until we close them, we are caught in life's race and the emotional fallout that comes with it.

We approach the day, and, more critically, our problems, like the exhausted mountain climber struggling up a treacherous slope. Nightfall looms, and he knows he must make his assault on the summit. Yet the harder he climbs, the more the summit eludes him. Fear sets in. Timing and judgment collapse.

In the eyes of the modern world, silent stillness looks like laziness. Outward activity is the conventional metric of performance. In reality, finding solace in the silent stillness is crucial to achieving potential.

Stop for five minutes. Close your eyes and breathe. Observe your every inhalation and exhalation. Breathe through your nose, if that is comfortable; it accelerates stillness. Draw your breath into your belly. You may notice that your shoulders are locked against your neck. Gently let them drop. Relax and rest into the rhythm of your breath. Good.

Silently, you stilled for a moment and looked in on your mind. You may have noticed many thoughts and feelings. Silent stillness is not about blocking these thoughts and feelings, but becoming aware of them. No longer were *you* the thought or feeling, but the observer of it.

Silent stillness provides the gap that enables us to discern one feeling, thought, or experience from another. Silent stillness opens that unspoken space that lives between the flow of life's moments, allowing previous thoughts, memories, feelings, or experiences to be different from the current ones. Because each moment gives emphasis to the next, this unspoken space gives life contrast, such as music is given life by the space between notes.

When you still, you encourage freedom. If you are jailed by your fears, heartache, worries, or resentments, how can you love life or love another? Freedom is the emphasis of life. It allows you to realize your life's vision and bring it to actuality.

In the same way as we find it difficult to be productive in a messy home or office, our minds find it difficult to be productive in an environment of misplaced thoughts and confusion. Silent stillness restores clarity. Like an excited crowd jamming the exits of a stadium, our thoughts and reactions jam our minds. Silent stillness gives structure to our mind's flow. It enables us to be dynamic and effective.

When you silently still, you build your brain and improve the way it works. Brainwave patterns improve and neuronal firing patterns synchronize. You build your prefrontal cortex and right anterior insula, the areas that control your self-awareness and emotional intelligence.[2] You literally strengthen circuits that are used and minimize those that are rarely engaged.[3]

Silent stillness gives us back the moment. It shifts our attitude and opens us to the reality that each of us is a potent moment in the turning of the world. As physics and mathematics now prove, each of us is an *event* in the framework of space-time, not a separate and isolated form.[4]

As you silently still, metacenteredness emerges. You discover gifts. More and more spontaneity propels your daily life. You laugh more, maybe cry more — though for joy, rather than despair. You see life's magic everywhere, reminiscent of childhood.

This shift in your heart is the beginning of your reversal. Your life's energy is undergoing an about-face in flow. The ancient Chinese called this the Great Reversal. Before, your reality was anchored outside your heart. It was a world of separation and opposition in which life was a series of in-groups and out-groups. People, events, and thoughts were either with you or against you. You occupied a landscape of fragments.

Now you anchor from within. Life again swells from your heart. Your potential, along with the hidden potential of the universe, begins to reveal itself.

With silent stillness comes peace.

To be at peace is to expand that split-second interval between circumstance and your reaction to it. Peace gives this split-second interval substance and quality. When you are metacentered, you occupy the space that interval creates. Rather than living the day-to-day routine through a mess of knee-jerk reactions, you respond with equanimity. You reply to life's challenges with centeredness and vision. Surprise and shock don't throw you as they once did, and insightful solutions meet difficulty with relative ease.

What at one time was a problem at work or home becomes a way of honing a skill. What was a fear becomes an opportunity for learning. Every problem holds hidden power. By asking "What can I learn?" we unleash that power.

The only true teacher is life. Success requires that you read and respond to the twists and turns in your unique path. Your future rests with you. The future is your opportunity. What you make of it is in your hands.

Discovering your life's vision is crucial. It is a rite of passage. Metacentering is the process of breaking free of conforming to the ways of others and seeking out your own life strategies.

To silently still allows you to embrace the reality that this is your life to live — no one else's. No longer are you a slave to your history and the insecurities that came with it. Your mind is freed. Now you implement your life vision rather than fight your history. Now vision creates reality.

Stillness and time

Life relies on time in order to fulfill itself. Over the framework of time, a tree grows roots to give it foundation and nourishment, and foliage to capture light and let it breathe. Time gives us the opportunity to create. Time provides the frame, which we fill with our potential; it allows us to work toward our vision and help others.

Our present relationship to time hinders our potential. We have lost our sense of time's natural cycle. We see time as necessary to maintaining schedules, rather than as a framework for touching beauty and realizing our vision. Many of us realize the value of time only when it is too late: "I should have done this," or "If I had a chance to do this again, I would have done that." It is easy to neglect the daunting reality that our time here on this beautiful planet with each other is but a moment — that the value of living will not be with us always. Through silently stilling we recognize that our opportunity is not later today or tomorrow; it is not waiting in some new year's resolution. It is now.

A beautiful way to silently still is to regularly remind yourself of your impermanence and the impermanence of those you love. This reminder holds your attention in the moment and allows you to see the magnificent in the every day. If you were to die tomorrow, what would you do differently today? Who would you choose to talk to and share your moments with? Appreciating that your life has a ceiling — that you are alive for a finite period of time — adds vast dimension to the moment. It ensures that you make the most of your life and not let it pass you by.

Freedom's Fury

How to Metacenter

Self

Part 2

Attitude

Three

L IFE IS TURBULENT. New challenges always lurk around the corner. You may feel perfect right now, but in a moment you might get an upsetting phone call, be told terrible news, or hear something that makes your blood boil.

The reality is that the dark events, more than the light events, are the ones that chisel success.

Success does not come to those who *react* to change, but *respond* to it. As the Buddha emphasized, we must accept unpredictability in order to see past it.

Embracing change makes a powerful statement. Threat becomes challenge. The darker the challenge, the more we are stirred to respond with inspiration and self-belief. Creative solutions are realized through an attitude of power. When we confront change with courage and right attitude, we cultivate the values necessary for success.

Viktor Frankl, a psychiatrist who survived a Nazi death camp, observed:

The experiences of camp life show that man does have a choice of action. There were enough examples, often of a heroic nature, which proved that apathy could be overcome, irritability suppressed. Human Beings can preserve a vestige of spiritual freedom, of independence of mind, even in such terrible conditions of psychic and physical stress.

We who lived in concentration camps can remember the men who walked through the huts comforting others, giving away their last piece of bread. They may have been few in number, but they offer sufficient proof that everything can be taken from a man but one thing: the last of the human freedoms — to choose one's attitude in any given set of circumstances, to choose one's own way.

Every day, every hour, offered the opportunity to make a decision, a decision which determined whether you would or would not submit to those powers which threatened to rob you of your very self, your inner freedom...."[5]

The only successful life strategy is to refuse to submit to those powers which threaten to rob us of our inner power, and make a dedicated effort to realize our vision.

A powerful motivator in confronting difficulty is to recall the beautiful and positive in our lives: the freedoms that democracy brings us, the clean air we breathe, the water we drink, and the fact that we can pass the day without going hungry. A life that is easy, filled with all the creature comforts one could ever wish for, can allow us to grow lax. We turn trivial mishaps into major upsets and inflate any task requiring real struggle into something insurmountable. Remembering what is working for us in our lives can be powerfully affirming. A metacentered habit is to spend a few minutes every morning recalling the beautiful and positive in your life. If practiced daily, this single habit can change your life. Try practicing this metacentered habit with your partner; it can enrich the relationship and extend your insight beyond what you have to feel grateful about.

By incorporating metacentering exercises in your daily routine, you lay the groundwork for moving from the ordinary to the extraordinary, where every waking moment becomes an opportunity for action and learning.

This is life. Living is celebrating existence. Every rock, flower, fish, and creek is testimony to the brilliance of the universe. Life is meant to motivate and inspire. A tree does not give up its growth in reaching for the sun in a season of heavy winds; it responds to the environment and journeys on.

Attitude is everything.

As Viktor Frankl's experience in a Nazi death camp illustrates, even in the most trying ordeals, we do have a choice of action.

Stabilizers

Cultivating right attitude creates structure in our lives. Without the miracle of structure, life could not exist. Everything from an atom to a one-celled amoeba to Mount Everest requires structure. Structure gives power a framework on which to function.

Within ordinary living, structure gives our lives a set of boundaries or guidelines within which we can envision a circumstance we feel inspired to realize and see it to actuality. The more we stabilize this structure in our lives, the more we metacenter our relationships, careers, and communities. Structure encourages stability, which allows our lives to remain firm, bracing us for those times that require our all.

A stabilizer is any action or thought that strengthens self-belief and dedication to our vision. One powerful stabilizer is silent stillness, which is described in Chapter Two. Taking the time to silently still every morning for 10 minutes can transform the day. Consider coupling it with the morning exercise of cultivating gratitude described above.

Another stabilizer involves changing a habit. Eating and drinking provide good examples. Gentle fasting, or excluding coffee, alcohol, or meat, can fuel focus. Altering diet also creates a healthier body, which strengthens mind and stamina.

Controlled breathing exercises are wonderful stabilizers. For example, the yogic technique of *Pranayam* can settle choppy emotions and recenter the mind within minutes.

Pranayam is a technique we can master quickly and execute behind our desk or at a traffic light.

Affirmations are also effective stabilizers because they pattern our thinking into behavior aligned with the fulfillment of goals. We create a circle of influence around our life that is inflected into our every interaction. A daily affirmation as simple, yet profound, as "I love myself for all my fallibility and beauty" or "I am rich in every vista of my life" can have a marked effect on the way we see and interact with the world.

By bringing focus to our ambitions, we invoke power. Stabilizing sends a message to our heart and our world that we are committed to our vision. It is no mystery that focus makes dreams reality.

We often forget that nature is also a powerful stabilizer. As we explore in Chapter Six, our lives would be far more satisfying if we stopped and remembered nature's rhythm.

Nothing energizes me like nature. By simply walking in a park, swimming in the ocean, or taking a look at the night sky, I harmonize with Earth and restore my awe for the universe. I believe it is in nature's interest that we awaken to our purpose and live it out. We are not separate from nature's miracle but an intrinsic part of it. Every animal and microbe on earth fulfills a vital purpose in balancing earth's harmony. We are no different. We all have a vital role to fill.

Chaos

Whenever I lose metacenteredness in times of trial, I look to nature for the answers. It is the most reliable teacher. Nature works with a primal clarity, in which everything has purpose and place. Look closely and you will discover that chaos is the basis of this melody.

The big bang — the birth of the universe — was the most chaotic event of all, yet the most wonderful. Just as chaos is fundamental to evolution, so, too, is chaos fundamental to our life. The rhythm of chaos works within us moment to moment. Our cells make a continuous journey of birth and death: they come into being, they fulfill their purpose, and they die. Within us, bacteria compete with bacteria, maintaining a healthy balance. Through chaos, one belief can come to replace an outdated belief. Arduous upheaval is often followed by awakenings. Chaos can be the herald of new life.

The ancient cultures understood that without chaos, the new could not emerge. This is why some personifications of the mother of life, beauty, and grace, like the Hindu goddess Kali, also personify death, terror, and destruction.

Chaos is not the enemy of metacenteredness, but a facilitator of it. Behind chaos lies an infinite order that is constantly seeking balance and, when necessary, collapsing order so that order can be restored. This collapsing of order occurs within our hearts and minds as much as it does in the world around us. The collapse of order is a critical part of the metacentering process, which we examine in Chapter Four.

Chaos is a force that can be channeled into our decision to be free.

As Viktor Frankl's concentration camp experience illustrated, right attitude was affirmed by the very circumstances which threatened to rob him of his inner freedom. His meta-centered attitude, and the metacentered attitude of others like him, was facilitated by the hellish events surrounding him.

The metacentered person uses chaos to drive his choice to succeed and be free; his decision is invigorated by the very adversity which surrounds him. Chaos drives him deeper into himself, and into the world, compelling him to respond with confidence, self-knowledge, and vision.

Surrender

Four

SURRENDER. IT MARKS the end of the familiar. It also marks a rare opportunity to break with the past. Surrender requires letting go of who you think you are and allowing life to show you. It is a rite of passage spanning the world's cultures that requires us to hand over control in exchange for revelation and self-knowledge.

Our view of surrender is flawed. We are a male-oriented society born of the belief that there is no power like willpower. To "give in" is to crumble. To "give up" is to fail.

This approach is unnatural. To stop and say a change may be at hand requires courage and intelligence. It is accepting the possibility that somehow our gifts and abilities may be better utilized. This is working harmoniously with circumstance, not dominating it.

Will is vital. However, it must be properly applied. When we allow insecurity to control us, we allow our day to become a matter of proving our worth to others, such as parents or friends. The paradise we work so hard to build becomes a paradise to satisfy the expectations of parents, partners, or society instead of our own hearts.

When we use our will to instead enjoy life and actualize our heart's dream, we apply power. This is dynamic participation, in which our inner world (our heart) and our outer world (our life) become aligned, working as one to achieve our goals.

Surrender moves in many ways. It can arrive with the illness of a loved one, or it can bring our own personal challenge, such as retrenchment or cancer. Or it may be that one day we simply cannot hold our will at bay any more. We grasp the frightening reality that we no longer want to be the person we have been working toward, that we have been maintaining an ideal of what we believe success to be, ignoring our heart. We realize that our life has been aligned to insecurity rather than power. Ironically, it is when we acknowledge "failure" that success can begin. Embracing this primal event — the moment when surrender becomes the only answer — marks the beginning of power, not the end of it.

Surrendering our smaller self is necessary if we are to become capable. Only upon Jesus' surrendering his life did he become Christ. Only through surrender could he resurrect. Only upon Prince Siddhartha's surrendering his smaller self did he become the Buddha.

Resistance

When we resist the new, we resist life. Surrender exists through birth, death, and renewal. To resist this cycle is to resist life. To reject a part of the cycle stops the entire cycle from working properly.

When we resist, we suffer. Resistance is motored by fear. What keeps us clinging to a destructive attitude, a belittling friend, or a dissatisfying job is insecurity. Resistance can be a sign that our perception is skewed — that we see life through a filter of self-doubt, rather than ability.

What we resist can become a doorway to power. Some of us long to be free of a relationship or job, yet when the opportunity arises, we do not act. Many of us live weighed down with unhappiness, yet when the promise of change arrives, we cower.

This is understandable. We like structure — it gives us security amidst the insecurities of the world. Yet, for many, our life structures are centered in insecurity, rather than in freedom. Like castles circled by walls, our defense structures are built out of our habits, fears, and insecurities to keep us safe from the unpredictable. Even our life's dream becomes flawed: we dream of a law degree or money, not to fulfill us, but to satisfy our need for approval. We continue to build our walls rather than tear them down.

When faced with surrender, we flee — yet surrender is, ironically, the very experience crucial to finding our way.

When we hide from ordeal, we hide from meaning. When we let go of one way of life in the pursuit of another, we foster faith and belief in ourselves.

We have a choice. We can make suffering torturous or useful. We can accept the pain and discern its value, or we can allow it to eat at us.

Here lies a forked road. We can decide to close our heart and batten down our will, or we can take a road less traveled, where the destination is unknown — but where we know in our hearts a worthwhile place awaits.

Faith

Faith is a battered concept in our modern world. Over time it has become a vehicle to carry our insecurities. Faith has become a life-buoy. We have come to see the wrongs or evils of the world as the work of higher purpose or chaos, rather than as an invocation to envisioned action.

Somewhere, faith lost its power and became a shell of what it was. Fear has come to rule faith, with freedom nowhere to be found.

Sometimes faith, like willpower, can be used to support a life that does not make us happy. Pseudo-faith is wielded by many as a weapon against change, when it is this very change that may be necessary to open our hearts or show us a better way.

We stifle power when we seek to control what our journey is, rather than allow life to show us.

Faith demands commitment. It requires us to quest beyond the safe and dependable. It requires us to trust.

Our society sees faith and logic as mutually exclusive, like oil and water. Yet the two are one. They emerged from the same desire to understand the world around us. When used properly they enrich each other, moving us closer toward wisdom and wonder. They work together like interweaving threads.

When used properly, logic gives definition and meaning to faith. One empowers the other — like lovers.

When we use them incorrectly, we turn not just faith, but also logic into a painkiller. With faith, we seek a higher power to rescue us, rather than empower us. With logic, we limit our potential by looking for excuses instead of looking for purpose. We come to accept a situation rather than ask how we can better it; as if it is normal to be in a job that is a drag, natural to be unfit, acceptable to be dissatisfied with life.

We let our world turn on blame. We seek to discover why a terrible event happened without inquiring how we can learn from it; we seek to blame something in our world — a disease, a person, a competitor, a country, a religion — rather than ask how we can gain wisdom from the experience.

Perhaps you know the story of the Odones, Augusto and Michaela and their little boy, Lorenzo. Leading up to Christmas 1983, Lorenzo, a gentle, sensitive boy, started having violent temper tantrums and auditory processing difficulties. Very quickly, his behavior became increasingly abnormal. Tests were done, but a cause could not be found.

In May 1984, the boy had further tests, after which the doctor revealed the worst:

Doctor: Lorenzo has a disease called ALD, adrenoleukodys-trophy. ALD is an inborn error of metabolism that causes a degeneration of the brain — it affects only males usually between the ages of five and ten. Its progress is relentless. All boys with ALD die usually within two years of diagnosis.

Michaela: And there are no exceptions?

Doctor: I am sorry.

Michaela: Are you absolutely sure?

Doctor: Yes.

That night Augusto read up on the disease at the library. A typical description of a boy who suffers ALD reads something like this:

Hyperactive, inattentive for two months; progressive withdrawal, mutism, and unsteady gait by four months; visual loss and quadraparesis by six months; blind, deaf, decorticate posture by eight months; death at nine months.[6]

Augusto and Michaela did not simply accept the prognosis, go home, and prepare for the worst. They investigated the disease and tried to discover why a cure was so elusive. They were not doctors by any measure. They were simply people with, as Augusto put it, "simple questions." They knew they had a five-year-old son who would be dead within fifteen months or so after suffering tremendously. A white coat saying "we know what we are doing" and "incurable" offered no solution to their pain. So they immersed themselves in everything they could find about the disease. They even brought the best minds on ALD from around the world to think-tank a solution, and by the time they were on their second mortgage, Augusto discovered the solution — regarded by the scientific community as "a beautiful piece of biochemistry." Augusto and Michaela found purpose amidst the darkest circumstance. They discovered the cause of the disease and a remedy — now known as Lorenzo's Oil. They saved their son and the sons of many others. Had it not been for the Odone's courage and determination, doctors would still be saying "incurable," and boys would still be dying agonizing deaths.

Logic

Imagine how life could be if we found purpose in the face of tragedy and resurrected the faith that we could make a difference in the outcome.

When we fail to seek understanding from trial, meaning is lost. Again we seek rescue by ill-reason rather than courage. We become logic's slave rather than its master. We misuse reason to find shelter in tragedy rather than freedom. Reasons can be useful — they help us to understand and work with life — but we often use them to sustain our complacency with the way things are.

The reality of surrender demonstrates that we are not in total control. Nor can we ever be. We are a part of nature, not masters of it. Scientists continue to discover that the deeper they dig, the more life reveals its beautiful mystery.

We stifle power when we seek to control what our journey is, rather than allow life to show us.

Faith coordinated with logic is the metacentered response. Adversity and hardship are not roadblocks to happiness but gateways.

Faith and logic live when we see potential behind circumstance. Like seeing brilliance behind the symmetry and function of a flower, faith and logic require that we see the symmetry of our lives in the eye of a moment. For instance, an argument between two people is not simply a venting of anger; it is a gateway to understanding, resolving differences, and improving communication.

Here lives meaning. No longer are we thrown by circumstance; we become responsive. We engage, not confront; we work with adversity, not struggle against it. To have faith and be logical is a place in which we sense our eternal part in the rhythm of the moment.

Life is mountainous; it holds both jubilation and trial. It requires stamina and courage.

Faith and logic are made strong when we use them to move ahead despite our fear.

Courage — one of the most respected and noble words — would not exist were it not for fear. Courage doesn't demand that we kill fear; it demands that we befriend it. Every fear holds a teaching. Overcoming fear, and learning by it, are necessary to wisdom and success.

It is important to remember, especially in hard times, why we are braving the struggle, holding the vision we are working toward, and overcoming the dissatisfying situation we are leaving behind.

Metacenteredness does not occur overnight. It develops slowly in a gritty fight with our insecurity and circumstance. Like any cycle of nature, it is a natural process. A bird leaves the nest only when it has found its wings. Metacenteredness develops and moves us toward success when we are ready for the responsibilities that come with it.

Every living thing has an itinerary of natural potential. Every human being has the opportunity to achieve special things in unique and wonderful ways. Like the bird struggling for flight, the harder we fight for success, the faster we attain it. Determination buys reward.

Providence

Five

A RE YOU READY to listen to your intuition instead of your fear? As the myths of the hero instruct, sometimes we must let go of what we believe life to be, or the assumption that we know where we are going, in order for life to show us.

We cannot master life by trying to understand it. We cannot preempt life. Mastery is beyond rationality.

To metacenter is to move into life — to become it.

A Zen student once asked his master:

"Sensei, tell me the secret of life."
The old teacher replied:
"Walk on."

Success does not reward the imitators — those who walk the well-worn path. The well-worn path tells of fear and resistance to the unfamiliar. Life rewards those who find their own way.

To step beyond the day, looking toward dreams and hidden aspirations, is a brave thing. The path of individuality speaks of creativity. It is a journey of belief and courage.

Your path

Each of us has a path that will require choices, offer opportunities, and impose burdens. When we truly commit to our path, we unleash events that help us to actualize our dream. Sometimes these events can manifest as a circumstance — a chance meeting, a timely phone call, or an unexpected opportunity — other times they can manifest as a dream or insight. Augusto Odone's discovery into the cause of ALD came to him in a dream while he was sleeping at his library table, exhausted by the ordeal to save his son.

It is not unusual to hear great achievers attribute part of their success to coincidence, luck, serendipity, or invisible hands — to a coordinating field operating beyond ordinary sight. The more we engage our vision and commit to it, the more we activate events within this coordinating field.

This coordinating field is like an electrical grid built around each of us. The more we quest, the more we generate coordinated events.

When people fail their dreams, lulled by temptations and societal pressure, they come to believe providence is an event limited to a handful of moments. No, it is our way of living that has made providence scarce. Whether you call it destiny, fate, karma, or kismet, the concept spans every culture and wisdom, reflecting the natural unfolding of coordinated events. The word providence not only means care through grace, but also preparation through foresight. Providence is ever-ready to coordinate our vision to our lives. The more we engage our dreams, the more we allow providence to assist us.

The Epistle of James in 2:15-26 says this:

Faith by itself, if it is not accompanied by action, is dead.... Show me your faith without deeds, and I will show you my faith by what I do.

Providence requires action. It is powered by our unrelenting commitment. The experiments of J.B. Rhine at Duke University demonstrated that our state of mind, despite being at a distance from the object it is seeking to influence, does affect outcome. Enthusiasm and an optimistic attitude help ensure a positive outcome, while, conversely, a negative outlook is detrimental to outcome. One's ability does transcend time and space.[7]

Cut off from nature, blanketed by concrete and sirens, we find it easy to forget that we are miraculous. You are a gift. Your very existence sounds a note in the melody of the world, and without you, the melody would be different.

By refocusing on nature, you invite the primal forces that drive it to work with you. Deserts, oceans, and mountains become your affirmation for empowered action.

Providence rewards courage. It requires that you work with the unknown and unexpected — not fight or flee it. Fear controls you when you believe that if you do not do as you are told, you will not be loved; or that if you do not do as those who have gone before you, you will fail; or if you risk, you will suffer.

Fear kills power. Remember: to listen to fear is to react — not respond. Approaching darkness with caution is sensible; not entering darkness at all is something else entirely. The hands of providence are tied when you tie yourself to your fear.

When you metacenter, you revolutionize your life; your every action is sheathed by vision. Life cooperates, conspiring for your success. People see it — you feel it. You become a cocreator with providence, working together with circumstance, not at war with it.

Providence is driven by love. It is ignited through faith and the undying belief that we can forge a life for the betterment of self and the world.

Love is the effect of being metacentered. When you cultivate love within, you create harmony in your world; when you cultivate love in your world, you nourish your heart.

You walk your path for the world to the same extent you walk it for yourself. Your decisions make an impact on the world. Your every action or inaction through temperament, consumption, and work either nurtures or destabilizes metacenteredness. You make an impact. Two revolutionary discoveries in mathematics called fractal geometry and chaos theory explain, through a concept called the Butterfly Effect, how the smallest act on one side of the earth can have a momentous impact on the other. Like the wisp of a butterfly's wings, your words, deeds, and silences can manifest a hurricane or miracle. You make a difference. Every thought, idea, action and non-action counts.

You not only improve your life when you cultivate love, you also strive for all.

You metacenter when you see your needs and the needs of your community as one.

Providence pervades every part of life, from giving birth to playing football, from clinching the deal to growing closer with family, from effectively identifying and serving life's needs to truly helping and supporting the needs of others.

As metacenteredness increases, so does providence. Providence fosters events that facilitate a metacentered life. The more metacentered you become, the more you are propelled by providence.

The Rise of Anger

Six

LIFE DIES WITHOUT anger. When we acknowledge our anger, we acknowledge our power. Without anger, we would not have the impetus to propel ourselves to new dimensions: we would tolerate inequity, we would accept injustice, and we would allow our lives to waste away.

Without anger, we would become content with a sick status quo: a selfish husband, an unjust government, a greedy company. Anger is the force of breaking through what no longer works, making room for a better way.

The gods of the ancient world that embodied power often represented destruction. They gave shape to the forces that bring transformation. Anger is this force. It invites freedom and change. When we open to our anger, we rise beyond it. We feel the power of our uniqueness — our individuality — and the satisfaction that comes with having braved the struggle to achieve it.

It feels good to speak your heart and stand up for what you believe. To live effectively, you must allow feeling to move through you. You cannot control feeling, it swells from deep places. Success means working with feeling and seeking to understand it, not to suppress it.

Your anger rises from the same place as your instincts. Your instincts — such as survival — support your drive to succeed and be free.

Each of us is an emanation of nature; a reality we tend to forget when we are immersed in the complexities of city life. Nature works and evolves by achieving a harmonious interplay of one organism with another. When we fall out of harmony with our life, anger develops. Anger marks an opportunity to move back into the ecosystem of life — the place where we function powerfully and harmoniously in ourselves and the world around us.

Harmony is achieved when we befriend anger.

Often, anger is the result of friction that develops between where we are and where, in our hearts, we yearn to be. We all get angry at times with a circumstance, friend, relationship, or job. How we deal with our anger is the key.

Anger develops when we do not assert ourselves. Often we tolerate circumstances to avoid the pain of confrontation and conflict, only coming to realize later that we are no longer content. How many times have you held your tongue only to ruminate later that you should have spoken your heart? The more we deprive ourselves of life — of freedom and choice — the more we fuel anger.

Anger is a productive inner force that attempts to push us back toward equilibrium, peace, and power. It seeks to rectify what we choose to ignore.

The anger within is a part of the primal within. By accepting anger and trying to work with it, these primal forces become allies in the battle for individuality and strength.

Demons, darkness, and all things terrible from mythology have been shut out of modern life. But in shutting out the darkness, we lose our way to mastery. Our dreams, our mythology, and our religion use the symbols of darkness to depict the psychological transformation that occurs within every one of us. Our demons are friends in disguise; they embody what we must confront if we are to be free.

Until you find the courage to confront and master your anger, you will be a slave to it.

Your anger is attempting to reconnect you to what is important. It is a feeling that seeks to realign you with truth. When you feel hurt or angry, it is because you are in pain. This pain is real. You must listen to it, not suppress it. Anger is the gateway that takes you back to freedom, not destruction. When you ignore it — when you shut it out — that is when it becomes destructive.

Irrespective of culture or creed, anger has always had its place. The universality of anger is testimony to its value, not its destructiveness. Because anger, like love, is universal, we can gain much by examining how other cultures of the world master it.

When we embrace this world truth, anger loses its menacing personality and becomes a force universal to all that seeks to bring us together, not rip us apart.

Your anger's potential

Intuition, insight, and inspiration are vital to working with anger.

When you use your intuition, insight, and inspiration, every response to change and crisis becomes a dynamic invention of the moment. When you are metacentered, you do not act from what has been or what you have seen, but from what you are seeing. Only in this metacentered place can the demands of the moment be met. It is the place where silent stillness plays its part, and anger becomes a natural opportunity to realign circumstance and attitude.

When you are metacentered, inspiration, insight, and intuition move electrically. You no longer meet another — you connect with another; you no longer speak to another — you engage another.

The more cut off we become from our natural potential, the more exposed we become to anger.

As we saw in Silent Stillness, each one of us is an event in the fabric of space-time. When we lock into life's daily tug of war, we relate to ourselves as somehow less than the measure of our potential. We see ourselves as separate, outside life's flow.

Your very existence is a state of ability. You are eternally in a state of electric movement. You move with the moment of life. And in the metacentered state, you see that the moment of life moves with you.

As a Zen master instructed his student:

The Buddha has no fixed forms. As he has no abiding place anywhere, no one can take hold of him, nor can he be let go. If you seek Buddhahood by sitting cross-legged, you murder him.[8]

As you work with your anger, you begin to see that just as you are a part of life's flow, so, too, is the moment around you.

Metacentering draws you closer to this eternal place. Such is the effect of nature on consciousness — it draws you toward that place where you become an event in the turning of the universe, and the universe becomes an event in the turning of you and your destiny.

Here the day-to-day blooms. Anger becomes an opportunity for addressing what no longer works: an old attitude, a misunderstanding, an ineffective way of doing things at the office. You become a gifted mother or father. You become an inspired manager. You become a true friend. You fill with humanity and express this creatively, every waking moment, in the many ways there are to communicate more richly with your children; in the many ways there are to enhance and develop your business; in the many ways there are to help your community.

The only limitation to improvement is the limitation you place on yourself. When you see your anger as bad, you restrict the opportunity for renewal. You miss what it means to truly share and grow with another. You lose the opportunity to find exciting solutions at work and home. You lose a timeless chance to strengthen the bond with your child.

In awakening to your metacenter, you locate the magical land alluded to in world mythology. You achieve the quest and come to realize the insight in Christ's observation that the kingdom is spread out upon the earth and people do not see it. You have possessed the Buddha nature from the beginning.

The world is perfect. It reflects everything that we are and everything that we are not: both beauty and cruelty, brilliance and ignorance, selfishness and compassion. Through that rich reflection the world shows us how we can aspire to be something more. What more can we ask of reality?

By seeing the shortcomings of the world and glimpsing its potential, we give birth to vision. The world's suffering inspires our hearts and compels us to reach further within. How could we learn about love, and feel the enrichment that follows from having applied those lessons, if the world were already the sum total of our ideals?

It is through what love is not that we discover what love is. Anger is very often the stepping stone to reclaiming this vision. Like inspiration and insight, anger rises from deep places and shares a unique heritage with these precious gifts. Anger is the servant of insight. When used properly, anger becomes a tool for inciting right action and creating opportunity.

Metacenteredness is the treasure for having endured the struggle of dying to your old ways of seeing your life and the world and being reborn as a capable and radiant human being.

Whether you are atheist or mystic, Muslim or Jew, being metacentered is knowing that day to day, moment to moment, you hold eternity, and your actions are inspired by this golden reality.

The words of Christ in the Gospel of Thomas enforce the message of many masters:

> *If your leaders say to you, "Look, the Kingdom is in heaven," then the birds of heaven will precede you. If they say to you, "it is in the sea," then the fish will precede you. Rather, the Kingdom is inside you and it is outside you.*[9]

Christ occupied this place of mind when he said:

> *I am in the Father and the Father is in me.*[10]

The same message is echoed in the instruction of a teacher to his student, immortalized by the ancient Indian *Upanishads:*

> *From me all emerge, in me all exist, and to me all return.*[11]

These words tell of the metacentered state. The purpose of the lives of these holy men, and of lives like theirs, was to emphasize that their experience of life's truth could be yours as well.

Working with anger

Anger releases force. As you give voice to your anger, life becomes a little chaotic. But chaos brings breakthrough. Chaos is the language of nature at its most primal and creative. Sometimes arid circumstances must be turned to become fertile again.

Be gentle with yourself. Do not force the boundaries of your life. Allow for space and solitude. Let those around you know that you would appreciate some room. Do not disassociate from your anger: stay aware and keep breathing. Acknowledge how you feel and stay forward-focused.

Stay aware of the big picture and do not let a small problem become a big one. Be mindful of the tendency to turn the insignificant into a mountain. Do not suppress your anger, or you will make a productive force destructive. Stay gently aware of inner turmoil, but keep moving.

As sure as the new day dawns, so will your night of darkness break with a new horizon.

Try to silently still. A personal set of words, such as a mantra or prayer, can be helpful. Such words provide support and structure to the inner journey. Mantras and prayers have been used for thousands of years in accelerating freedom — and they work.

Relax. Have some fun. Immerse in activities that fill you with joy. Kick a ball with a friend, plant a tree, draw something inspiring, write a poem, play some music, or sing your favorite tune.

Massage and exercise are also extremely helpful. Both clear blocked forces and help us to relax.

If you are in a social mood, spend time with people who provide a light environment, but who don't try to fix you. Even if you feel like being alone, spending time with others can be uplifting.

Perhaps keep a list of reminders, or prompters, in your purse or wallet for those times when you feel turmoil looming.

Structural supports to metacentering do not include cigarettes or alcohol. Although they might provide an escape from hurt, they jeopardize breakthrough. Alcohol and cigarettes drain power. They kill metacenteredness. It may not be necessary to eliminate alcohol and cigarettes so long as you consume from a place of want rather than need, and in moderation rather than excess.

Nevertheless, it is important to eliminate dependency. Do not torture yourself in the process; as you become more metacentered, the desire for fixes will disappear. Be sure to do whatever you can to eliminate dependency, for nature assists only when you assist yourself.

If you are dependent on smoking, drinking, or overeating, you may find the support of a group focused on achieving a common goal very affirming. Support groups such as Alcoholics Anonymous, Weight Watchers, or a smoking cessation program often make the difference in overcoming a destructive habit.

Exercise and diet are also important to metacentering. We all recognize the common sense inherent in the saying,

"A healthy body is a healthy mind." Metacentering involves all aspects of your life. If one part of a tree is unhealthy, it restricts the growth of the other parts.

Exercise lifts attitude. The best approach to maintaining a good exercise routine and a healthful diet is common sense and dedication.

Nature

One of the most powerful aids to working with anger is to experience nature. Engage the wonder of the natural world and I promise you will be inspired. The natural world brings you back to your natural rhythm. Looking at the moon across a congested urban landscape can help us remember what is and what is not important. Listening to the rain dancing on the roof can be a lullaby. Swimming in a river, lake, or ocean can be electric.

Looking to nature is one of the most effective ways to metacenter. The more we accommodate nature, the more we align.

When we treat nature with complacency, we treat ourselves with complacency. When we treat it with respect, we embrace our primal origins and our place in life's scheme. The degree to which we respect nature reflects the degree to which we respect ourselves.

Reconnect with nature regularly. Focus on things that revitalize you — whether taking a walk in the park, spending some time with the night sky, or listening to a recording of natural sounds in your office. Even watering a plant on your windowsill can be a rewarding act. Ultimately, though, take time to rest in the natural rhythm of the mountains, forest, desert, or sea.

Change is nature's fundamental. Anger marks our resistance. It can be frightening to address our anger; to speak our heart or tackle a trying circumstance. Yet to live effectively, this is precisely what we must do.

Embracing the way of renewal is a major step to mastering anger. Fear inhibits freedom. It suffocates creativity. By seeing your life as an event, as a sequence of flowing moments, you come to see not just the beauty, but also the necessity in change. You accept and master even the most trying challenges.

With a little work, anger is converted to a motivating driver. Force once invested in fearfulness now becomes invested in action: worry converted to hope, and fear converted to vision.

Suffering

Seven

S OCIETY NEITHER RESPECTS nor learns from those who suffer; it pities them. How sad, because pity is the last thing a sufferer needs. Many of us try to smudge the sufferer from our memories because their misfortunes remind us of our own vulnerabilities.

We must embrace the suffering and destitute to overcome our own fears and deepen our humanity. To be with another in his or her suffering is a privilege and a blessing.

Because it takes courage for a person in pain to let in someone else, suffering can cause caustic loneliness. As a person is swallowed by his or her pain and fear, the day-to-day world moves on, oblivious. To know that someone cares can be deeply affirming.

Every one of us has suffered and will suffer again. When it is your turn, whether a small issue or a life-threatening one, you have two choices. You can see the pain from a place of fear and resistance, or you can make it an opportunity to journey deeper. Although fear is natural, you must decide whether you want to feed it or learn from it. Suffering can mark a rare opportunity for endings and beginnings.

Many who have suffered come to see their suffering as meaningful. It is not unusual to hear people say during or after an ordeal that their pain opened unexpected doorways. Suffering can take us to deeper, more worthwhile places.

Death's possibility can become revelation's passage. Through this passage we can decide to be teachers. Every person we engage — nurse or niece, student or son — can be lifted by our courage and grace. Through rising to meet ordeal, we provide an example to others and inspire them.

To suffer bravely is the ultimate experience of humanity.

Suffering bravely gives others the faith and courage to face their own fears. You have the opportunity to discover a rich part of yourself and help others. It is a path paved in dignity and purpose.

I have never forgotten my mother's smile on the morning she was to undergo a mastectomy. She was in mortal fear, and yet, as she was wheeled down the hall for her operation, she beamed a sunrise back at us. Her courage that morning invoked renewed determination in my own life.

Suffering can allow us to fulfill a very deep part of destiny. It can mark a return to meaningful life and open the miraculous.

If you are experiencing the approach of death, you have the power to help another in an invaluable way by deciding how you will suffer. In confronting your illness with equanimity and courage, you leave an indelible mark on the memories of those around you. Your memory will support and sustain them for the rest of their lives and help them when their time comes. This is one of the most defining and challenging paths of all.

We are all teachers until our final breath; then, like a tree releasing its fruit, our memory lives on through those we have touched.

When metacentered, you embrace your suffering. You come to see that like the marriage of the moon to the sun, life would be nothing without suffering reflected against it.

Energy

Eight

E NERGY, LIKE THE universe, is infinite. We do not know what energy is: we only know some of its attributes. Like a prophet speaking about God, a scientist can describe the behavior of energy, but not its source.

Living energy is moving in and around you every moment. When you die, you lose form, but the energy you encompass does not cease to exist.

Energy embodies all: it is the canvas, the paint, the brush, and the artist.

Energy is animated by cooperation and conflict. The relationship between these two forces is what we have come to know as the tension between opposites. It runs through the world's religions and mythology, represented in sacred symbols such as the yin and yang, the Hindu gods Shiva and Shakti, the cross, the ancient swastika,[12] and the Star of David.

Each of these forms symbolizes the play of life's energies: the meeting of the upright with the inversed, the horizontal with the vertical, man with woman, heaven with earth. Each depicts the way of life's force. Each is a key to understanding life and our relationship to it.

All these symbols describe the metacenter, and when used properly, guide us to mastery. What they represent helps us to rise beyond the day-to-day and discern purpose and wisdom.

When you are metacentered, both you and the world work together. When you respond to circumstance instead of react to it, you take responsibility for who you are becoming.

Response involves a committed engagement with circumstance in which we ask of the situation: "What is there to learn from this event?" and "What is the best outcome?" Responsibility is the effect of being responsive — in which we work with circumstance rather than react to it. The next time you are about to launch into an argument, first ask yourself how you may have contributed to the miscommunication or misunderstanding.

By continuously asking the question "what is there to learn from this event?" you achieve responsibility and come to live in a way authentic to you: the metacentered way.

The metacentered way is found in independence, not compliance. In complying with others instead of listening to your heart, you undermine your potential.

When you look at yourself in the mirror, you see a haircut and a face that needs either makeup or a shave. But if you stop and look beyond that, you can see an example of nature's beauty and intelligence: your face and body have evolved to work with poetic genius in your environment.

For example: take a deep breath, shut your eyes for a moment, and identify something that is worrying you — a difficult boss, a silent spouse, a disloyal friend, an out-of-control credit card balance.

Next, take that worry and write it on a piece of paper. When we identify the power behind discordant feeling, we defuse it — like knowing an enemy in battle. Now take another deep breath and ask: "How can I act on this?" Furthermore, "Do I need to act on this?" That is, ask if this discordant feeling requires an outward response, such as dealing with the person this feeling concerns. Ask if it requires an inward response, such as deciding that the event is perhaps not as large as it first appeared and that your discordant feeling has been amplified by your own history of rejection, betrayal, or hurt.

Wisdom waits within you; your feelings are messengers.

The more metacentered you become, the more you realize that love and ability are one.

Taking responsibility for your power and individuality is the key. The universe is eternal — yet unless you live, a vital part of the universe will never live. You form an aspect of infinity and all that makes it mysterious, noble, and powerful. If you die to your dreams, a part of the universe will die with you. If you rise to your dreams, part of the universe will rise with you.

Freedom's Adventure

The Metacentered Life

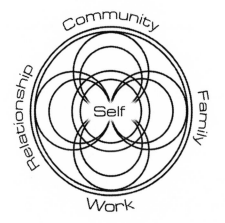

Part 3

Metacentered
Relationship

Nine

THE WORLD'S RELIGIONS and shamanic cultures
exclude marriage from the path of the astute spiritual
practitioner for a reason. Relationship is one of the most
demanding challenges in the experience of living. The
challenge of relationship has led to two experts on the art of
living and relationship to proclaim that relationship is an
ordeal and a *crucible* in which we come to awaken and
integrate the finest aspects of our hearts and minds into the
field of life. Relationship is an art in which the *practitioners* are
engaged in a journey of mutual awakening and enablement,
each empowering the other to plunge deeper into their hearts
and into the world.

When I left Sydney to write *Freedom's Way,* a friend and I
opened a café in the country. It provided an opportunity to
observe and interact with many couples in a very natural, un-
contrived setting. Out of at least a thousand couples, two stood

out as metacentered. It was obvious that these two couples had a resonance of mutual awakening and enablement. One couple, the Clarkes, were in their late seventies and living in a retirement complex in the mountains: they were grandparents and spoke about their lives together with delight and play. The second couple, the Johanssons, at first seemed so enamored with each other that I thought they were a new match on their first romantic weekend away. I came to discover they were the parents of two teenage children and in a deeply committed relationship. The common set of qualities between these couples was that they had a thirst for living, they smiled, they forgave, and each humbly embraced the reality that every day was an opportunity to learn something new about themselves, each other, and the world. Both couples were effervescent, and they spoke with a certain relish about their past and their lives together. They were not just adventurers of the world, but themselves.

The metacentered partner is not born this way; they become that way. They adopt the discipline of allowing themselves to be vulnerable, and they drop the assumption that their viewpoint is the only reality. They live in accord with Einstein's observation that no reality is objective. Every person's reality is an authentic view of the world, and every person's ability to love and be loved is built around their own personal, authentic view. Every person's heart, dreams, fears, and insecurities are molded around their unique history and genetics. The metacentered partner shares their reality and allows a third reality to emerge.

The miracle of relationship is that it is a passage unlike any other that bridges two people who are compelled to connect and awaken beyond their pre-relationship view of self and the world. They literally grow beyond who they were and come to see self, each other, and the world more expansively with continuity and color.

The opportunity of a metacentered relationship is excitingly new, thanks to the freedoms of modern living. Psychiatrist Erwin Maslow's hierarchy of needs is famous. In it he illustrates how the individual and society operate on a pyramid of needs necessitated by the primal need of survival. As each need is satisfied, the next, more subtle need can be satisfied. At the foundation of the needs scale is body: the need fixed on achieving what literally enables us to survive — things such as shelter and food. Once the immediate need of the body is satisfied, the individual and society seek to satisfy mental and emotional needs, leading ultimately to spiritual need at the top of the pyramid. As our modern society has become materially satisfied, our needs have evolved from simply requiring stable support to thirsting for a partner who provides spiritual sustenance. The aspirations and opportunities of relationship become vessels not just for creating a home but also for transforming ourselves and each other. With this new hyperintense expectation around the exciting challenges of relationship, three qualities of loving become imperative: trust, courage, and vision.

Trust

Trust is earned. Trust is forged through anger, honesty, and self-knowledge. Trust requires not just faith in our partner, but faith in ourselves. How can we trust another if we cannot trust ourselves and have faith in our own ability to find happiness and be free? Love starts within. Trust requires us to be willing to emerge out of our zone of safety and have faith in who we are and what we can become. The presence of the metacentered partner enables each partner to keep striving outward, compelled by love. Our zone of safety is that place within our current reality, built throughout our personal history, which tells us what will ensure our survival. Our zone of safety is not an accurate picture of the world. It is framed by our experience of the world, and we know no different. Like a turtle, our reaction is to pull in our heads and use whatever emotional artillery we have to protect our boundaries. However, the very miracle of loving is constantly compelling us to do the opposite.

This degree of loving requires discipline. It demands that we do not become turtles and bring out the artillery, but rather use the life skills discussed in *Freedom's Way* and books like it to ensure we serve the relationship and act responsively, not reactively. Relationship is an art because it requires a constant forging of ourselves, not our partners. A metacentered relationship is never achieved; it is in a constant state of being and becoming, ever deepening, in which the two people who make it learn about self, other, and world. This process of deepening is enabled through the ongoing development of trust. Honesty, communication, and the willingness to be vulnerable is imperative. Trust is developed when we emerge from our zone of safety. We must step into our vulnerability in order for something beautiful to emerge.

Courage

Because relationship has become an "ordeal" and a "crucible" in which we come to awaken and integrate the finest aspects of our hearts and minds into the field of life, it requires a life myth of equal power to guide us.

A beautiful story is told about King Arthur and his knights called La Queste del Saint Graal or The Quest for the Holy Grail.[13] Picture Camelot: perched, as some say, on a misty, rugged coastline on a remote cliff top called Tintagel, where the winter wind feels like splinters. The sun had all but sunk below the horizon and King Arthur and his knights were seated at the Round Table, preparing to drink and feast. As the wine was being poured and the knights were laughing, sharing tales of bravery, the flares suddenly dimmed, and despite the closed doors, a gentle breeze blew. Thunder cracked, intense light splintered the room, and out of nowhere appeared the Grail, covered by a delicate, satin cloth and carried, so the myth says, by angelic miracle. It emitted a gentle glow, and a heavenly fragrance floated through the room. The Grail levitated for a moment over the Round Table, holding the knights' gaze. Then, as suddenly as it had appeared, it vanished.

King Arthur and his Knights were, understandably, ec-static. Each sat deep in awe. But then Sir Gawain stood up and pointed out that the vessel had been veiled, and he said, "Be-fore we drink, I propose that we each make a vow. I propose that we each go in search of the Grail and behold it unveiled, and that each of us enter the forest where he feels it darkest, and where there is no path." That proposal stays with me still: where it is darkest and where there is no path. I have always envisioned each of the knights riding hard toward the forest, the clash of hooves, the spray of mud, then alone, at the last moment, each umbrellas out and punches the foliage, swal-lowed by the darkness.

A relationship worth striving for is never handed to us. It is an initiation. I relate to the dark forest as ourselves when we puncture our zone of safety propelled by the vision of what the relationship can become. By having the courage to enter into the darkest parts of our interior, we can emerge awakened and renewed. The metacentered relationship is a quest, a modern day rite of passage. Every time you feel hurt or insecure around your partner, try to recall the message of this Grail myth. Chances are your hurt or insecurity has been amplified by your history. The fact that your partner enabled that feeling to emerge has created an opportunity by which you can plunge into your interior, silently still, and reflect on what motivated the hurt. Later, once the reactivity has diminished, talk with your partner and share your experience.

The other interesting part of this Grail myth is the initial appearance of the Grail. The Grail represents for me the vision we first have when we fall in love with our partner and become immersed in a luminous feeling of elation. We get a sense of who we are and who we can become through the experience of being together. It is this vision that compels the journey, the willingness to suffer the ordeal, and to make the relationship our crucible.

Vision

Even two thousand years ago, the Bible stated that "where there is no vision, the people perish."[14] In the metacentered relationship, the same advice applies. Vision, like the image of the Grail for the knights, drives the quest. The vision propels the couple to clarify desires, empower commitment, and overcome obstacles within self and world. With the distractions of modern living, one can easily be swayed from what is truly important. The Vision Driver for Relationship in Part 4 will help you ensure that your relationship remains aligned. If your relationship is in dire need of significant realignment turn to the Vision Driver for Wounded Relationship.

If your relationship eventually dies, never, ever feel it was a failure of your quest. Our minds are so easily split from the world, we are led to invest all our hopes and dreams in another, when ironically we must place this investment first in ourselves. So long as you do your best to stay metacentered, crucial knowledge and wisdom will be achieved to empower the next phase of your life.

The metacentered couple staunchly adheres to the vision they feel inspired to realize. They work at their togetherness, retain their passion for living, and work at being the custodians of a fulfilling relationship. They remember to smile, forgive, and accept their partner's fallibilities, and each acknowledges that the way the other sees the world is equally valid. The meta-centered partner works at changing himself, not his partner, and in so doing transforms the relationship and the way in which he interacts with the world.

Metacentered Family

FAMILY IS A neglected road to self-knowledge. We can gain great wisdom by being part of a family. We can forge meaningful connections with our parents and siblings. By discovering as much about ourselves and our world as our children discover about theirs, we can foster meaningful bonds with our children.

The courage to say no

Most family members like to avoid conflict. We see argument, anger, and resentment as disruptions to harmony instead of opportunities to deepen it.

However, it is through the arguments, the fury, and the resentments that we can learn to master our emotions and hone our ability to be responsive in daily interaction. We can learn to focus on the value of each relationship, rather than on blame and resentment. We can learn how to respect and address the cause of the conflict, rather than allow it to fester. And we can master valuable life lessons.

An important life lesson is mastering the skill of noncompliance. One of the most supportive things a parent or loved one can do is say no. We need to revive this practice of respect. We do not serve by complying with demand and saying "yes" or "no problem." We achieve nothing when we do something begrudgingly.

Sometimes we comply so much it becomes a habit. A habit of compliance is particularly insidious because we eventually grow into a weakened state. We come to live our lives through a language of compliance that we do not even know we are using. Feeling dies, as does, ironically, the relationship we have been trying to maintain.

By telling a loved one how you feel, you allow them into your world. You evoke their compassion and understanding, not reaction. By speaking with courage — with heart — worlds open.

We assume that we know what we want. We assume that we know what will make us happy, what will make us successful, what will make us loved. We shape our relationships and our lives on these assumptions. However, all these life assumptions are the products of our own mental and emotional arithmetic. Just because these assumptions have become our system for interacting with the world, does that make them accurate?

What if we are misreading a relationship through the lens of low self-esteem? What if we are wrongly measuring another's opinion or actions through the lens of arrogance?

What if we have forgotten what it feels like to love, be loved, and be happy? Like growing up in a foreign land, we can come to live by attitudes and beliefs that are not our own. It is very easy to come to a point at which we engage the world defensively, arrogantly, defiantly, or compliantly, and never even know it.

Courage is crucial to overcoming our life assumptions. It takes tremendous bravery to step beyond what we know. However, if we are to achieve metacenteredness and metacentered relations with our families, this is exactly what each of us must do. We must brave new ways of seeing and new ways of being.

Remember: your life is an event. Your life is an ever-turning process. How could your perception of self or your relationships be any different?

The faster you see that your perception is a process, the faster you will see beyond your current life assumptions.

Empathy

Caught in the rush of the day-to-day, it is easy to lose sensitivity and compassion.

However, when we lose touch with our feelings, we lose touch with ourselves and those we love.

Family offers one of the best opportunities for developing empathy. Because family was the bedrock of our reality during our formative years, it provides a powerful starting point for addressing inward change.

To forgive a friend or colleague with whom we don't share a life's time is easy. To forgive a mother, father, brother, or son with whom the relationship has become encrusted with misunderstanding and judgment is a heavier challenge.

The irony is that the angrier we are with a family member, the more we are likely to care for them. The anger has developed because of friction between where the relationship is and where we want it to be.

Challenging? Yes. But why would we continue to struggle against the emotional torrent and continue to endure the pain were this not so? If we could discern the truth that our compulsion to keep trying is motivated by care and could hold to this truth through the barrage of our own history and insecurity, we could evoke great change within ourselves, and — likely — within the relationship itself.

However, the purpose of this journey cannot be motivated by a need to have your mother, father, or sibling change. You must direct this need inwardly toward changing yourself.

Who knows where the resentments, frustrations, and hurt began? Who knows who initiated the cycle? To engage in a battle of blame is fraught with peril. Accusations and blame leech love of its potential.

We fall into the trap of judgment instead of staying focused on our love for one another and empathizing with each other's struggle — while at the same time not getting caught up in it.

Empathy is powerful. It is vital to success. Caught in the torrent of the day-to-day, we lose sensitivity and compassion. You help another and yourself by opening to another's pain.

Your sensitivity and compassion say to others, as well as to your own heart, that you are fellow travelers on life's journey.

The wisdom in vulnerability

Risk. Everything worthy and valuable to our civilization has been built on this principle. Rarely do we associate risk with being a healthy parent, son, daughter, or partner, even though it takes great courage to say "I was wrong" or "I love you."

To metacenter, you must be vulnerable. When you respect your vulnerability you can address the insecurity that has developed around it.

In modern society, sensitivity is a demonstration of weakness.

In reality, sensitivity is a demonstration of strength. When we close our hearts we lock out kindness and insight.

The ancient Delphi challenge to know thyself does not call for classroom philosophy. Know thyself calls for us to look inside our hearts and our histories. Know thyself is not so much a call for intellectual inquiry as a call for a brave descent into our hates, our hurts, our pains, our fears, and our dreams.

Until we address our fear, we will be overcome by it — we will continue to cast blame and make excuses that camouflage the real motive behind our inaction.

When we allow ourselves to be vulnerable we come to see that the barriers we believed blocked our paths to loving relationships are not barriers at all — they are self-limitations placed there by us.

When we look to our vulnerability instead of blindly defending it, we illuminate choices that were not visible before. When we admit our fallibilities, we transcend them. A meta-centered person knows that through understanding his own vulnerabilities, he can empathize with his family's. He accepts the reality of pain and fear. He knows that life is more productive and rewarding for the integrity he brings when conversing with his loved ones and with himself.

When metacentered, a person listens to her reactions and responses. She sees when action, comment, thought, or feeling is a product of caring or selfishness, confidence or worry, concern or callousness.

Every time the metacentered person makes a mistake, she refines her wisdom by asking, "What have I learned from this event?"

She treats her reactivity as the fodder for self-reflection. She holds to her vision of what it is to be a metacentered family member. She accepts that she has made mistakes, is making mistakes, and will make mistakes, and she knows these mistakes are refining her ability to love.

The metacentered person who at one time was defensive and insecure becomes increasingly self-assured and strong. Now every time she makes a mistake, she is one step closer to fulfillment, learning from her errors instead of hiding from them. Discordant feelings previously invested in protection now ignite self-awareness.

Parenthood

Even though you may not be a parent, you are nonetheless a mother and a father in a wider context. You are a custodian of the world's youth. Their attitudes, fears, and dreams are affected by the attitudes, fears, and dreams you convey as a member of society.

Children also are our custodians: every child can help us to remember the wisdom of innocence.

When we read the word *parenting*, we think immediately of children. However, parenting holds a hidden opportunity — it encourages us to reflect on our own childhood and trace how our mind developed.

How have your attitudes toward empathy, vulnerability, and imagination been shaped by your experiences as a child? More importantly, how have those experiences rippled through to the attitudes, prejudices, and beliefs you hold today?

Whether you are seventeen or seventy, this exercise can unearth realizations and present some fascinating opportunities to see your life anew. Parenthood is not only about how you parent — it is about how you were parented. Your experiences of being parented form an important step to metacenteredness because these questions guide you back to making decisions from your heart, rather than your history.

The rest of this chapter is not solely for parents, but for those of us who wish to look back and explore our own upbringing.

Parenthood is powerful. It gives purpose and joy.

At the same time, with privilege comes responsibility. Before every child lies joy, pain, and purpose. By choosing to be a parent, you accept the responsibility to support a child in her journey. You are a companion, guide, and confidante.

The effective parent teaches by action and example. We tell our children to obey, they see us do differently, and we wonder why they do not listen. The metacentered parent's motto is not "do as I say" but "do as I do."

You have the power to fill your child's life with self-belief and wisdom or drain it through insecurity and misdirection. Your attitudes are being noted just as your manners are. How you approach life — the trials, the joys — is your child's point of reference. For the early years, your view of the world — with all your insecurities and confidence, irks and joys — is their view of the world.

Metacentered parents know they are custodians of something precious and fragile, and crucial to the future of humanity. When you respect your child and appreciate that the primal wisdom of the ages lies within her as within you, you cultivate understanding and guidance in the relationship. When you look at your child, look beyond his day-to-day face, beyond her naughtiness — like looking "beyond yourself" in the mirror (discussed in Chapter Eight).

Recall this reality at least once a day, especially in the morning. It will help you to increase responsiveness, learn by reactivity, and interact with your child more constructively. Now you become the guardian of a living wonder.

The metacentered parent sees the relationship to her child as two souls traveling life's road together. Like fellow travelers, they exchange joy, support, and wisdom. The parent protects the child; the child protects the parent's heart. Both grow.

Innocence

By communicating with your children, you awaken the innocence within you. The word innocence means free, unhindered.

In our daily fight for prestige and a paycheck, we have lost touch with life's value. Seeing through the eyes of our children helps to open a world we have forgotten.

Vision springs from inspiration and insight. In modern life, these faculties are treated with disregard. To suffer a job, to look forward to Friday and dread Monday, is considered normal. To listen to your vision and to act on it is considered naive — or abnormally courageous.

Because we are products of reason, vision and insight have become irrelevant. We have created a world of the destitute visionary. However, as a modern society, we yearn for something more. Still we hesitate, fearing the consequences of surrendering to everything we believed we had to abandon. We hesitate because we fear that we won't be accepted, that we won't have enough money, and that — above all — we might fail after all.

Have you ever met a person who regretted their dreams?

We parent with power and help to renew our culture when we help our children hone talent and make the most of vision and insight. It is natural for children to work from their intuition, insight, inspiration, and imagination. They live by these natural modalities. Yet as adults we have banished imagination, inspiration, insight, and intuition. Anything outside our immediate field of sight and experience is treated with doubt.

In doubting, we close an Aladdin's cave, and we isolate ourselves from our children and our potential. The enthusiasm of our children is a place of richness to which we should all aspire.

The qualities embodied in our children — their questions, their observations, their thoughts — are treasures.

When a child speaks her heart, it pays to listen, and it pays to listen to the manner in which we respond. Our child's words are generally a reflection of our own heart's thought, without the trappings of control and inhibition:

"Daddy, why are you upset?" or "Mommy, why are you angry?"

Questions and observations springing from a child's lips tell of a beautiful and wise human being.

Your past or your child's present?

Less than a hundred years ago, children were treated with disregard, even disdain. They were seen, but not heard. They were even seen as sinful.

It would be naïve to believe that our society has freed itself from these shackles. As with every aspect of our inherited history, old ways lurk just below the surface.

These old ways rise in moments when we react under stress. Be ever aware of the reason behind your actions. When you scold your child, ask yourself whether you are responding or reacting to the circumstance.

A reaction is often fueled by the past.

For example, it is not unusual for a father to dole out the same punishment he received as a child. Mindlessly repeating what we were subjected to is human. Often when we get angry with our children, it is more because we are frustrated with our own inability to deal with the situation than because our children have misbehaved. Response embodies a constructive way of working toward a common goal with your child. For example, a father may ask his son, who dropped a toy on his sister, whether he saw the harm in his act. Together they work toward understanding.

As you learn to respond to your reactivity, you will make mistakes. It is important to acknowledge that you are fallible. One of life's joys is the experience of learning. Children are worthy teachers. Do not punish yourself by questioning whether you did the right thing. Respect your child, learn from the situation, and focus on deepening your relationship.

When we encourage children to speak their truth and express how they feel, we give them the self-worth and confidence to grow. It is important for us, as role models, to listen to the lessons we instill. We must lead by example. By choosing to be parents, we take additional responsibility to extend ourselves for the sake of our children.

In the same way your baby was endowed with the title of "daughter" or "son" at birth, you became endowed with the title of "mother" or "father." In becoming a family, all of you have new roles to fill and challenges to rise to. You would not be who you are were it not for that other.

The greatest thing you can do as a parent is to help your child develop his potential and self-belief, to give him the confidence to realize his dreams. Everyone has dreams — everyone has a vision of what they want their life to be. When we help our children to find their dream and act on it, we love.

Metacentered parenting means recalling our own insight, intuition, and imagination and doing our best to ensure that our children never lose these golden ways of relating to life, but instead learn how to apply them.

Metacentered Company

Eleven

BY OPENING TO the deeper potential of its people, a
company harnesses power. Business is beginning to grasp
that a successful company is one that sees itself as something
more than a supplier of products and services.

All the laws that apply to the metacentered individual apply to any group working with a common purpose. Life's way is
not restricted to the individual. Like a nation, a company lives
and breathes through the people who comprise it.

Like the components of an engine, each individual is relevant and necessary. Each brings skill, know-how, and insight,
and the performance or lack of performance of each individual
determines the company's success.

Until now, the world of business, like society, has focused
on the rational. We have suffered the delusion that the only
space outside the rational is the irrational. Holding this attitude, we severed ourselves from life's hidden language. Like
the individual, corporations have forgotten power's way. As
commercial players, we have lost sight of insight and innova-

tion, and we have desperately lost sight of the power and potential behind what it means to love and to profit.

People and passion

A company has hidden ability locked within it. Every individual helps to make the company. By suppressing the flame of the individual, we suppress a company's ability to profit and grow.

A company's success is directly proportional to the success of each of its people. A worried, stressed, or unhappy salesperson, call center consultant, accountant, or chief executive does not perform as effectively as she could.

If an employee is not metacentered, her decisions are not metacentered.

A company breathes through its people. If the employees' attitudes are sick, the company's initiative and drive suffer. If the successes and output of the individual are low, the successes and output of the company fall.

Employee and company, when metacentered, are one: each gives life to the other. When we neglect this fact, the needs and attitudes of the employees lose alignment with the needs and attitudes of the company. Potential becomes inhibited, output decreases, innovation diminishes, and market share erodes.

The degree to which metacenteredness is ignored by company and employee reflects the degree to which employee and company are out of alignment.

Through outdated reasoning and values inherited from the industrial revolution, we tend to see the company as separate from its people. Too easily we neglect the reality that a thousand employees are a thousand hearts. We forget that every employee holds fears and heartache, and every employee holds dreams.

Moreover, employees are the best resource for discovering new products or improving current ones. Every employee is a consumer and knows the product or an aspect of the product intimately. A company that makes razors has a company full of legs and faces; one that makes computers has a company full of users; one that makes mattresses has a company full of sleepers.

When a company fails to listen to its people, it fails to listen to itself. Arrogance and conceit hammer the first nail in the coffin of profit and creative potential. Slowly the company becomes one of decay and closed minds. Stagnation begins. The staff and administration dig in. An attitude of survival rules instead of an attitude of achievement and ability.

Ideas and initiative flourish with encouragement and support. When we welcome the radical or the new or simply provide a noncritical environment that invites questions and queries, we encourage innovation and excellence. We need to feel human at work. When we feel human, we rekindle passion.

Passion is everything. It fuels brilliance. It fuels strength. It fuels fortitude. It also fuels corporate survival and success in a viciously competitive landscape. Until passion infuses the blood of your company, it will remain an embryo of what it could become.

A simple test for assessing your personal passion is to sit, close your eyes, and take a deep breath. Drop your shoulders. Picture yourself in thirty years. Look back on your work and the products, services, and relationships you created: Are you satisfied with your accomplishments? Do you feel complete? Did you achieve and contribute in all the ways you wanted?

Apply this test to your company. How will your company, with its current vision, culture, and results, look thirty years from now? Will the company even exist? If so, how will the company, people, and the world have benefited?

Communication

Communication is the bedrock of a company. Communication is also fundamental to us as human beings. Yet we neglect the fact that to listen to others, we must first be able to listen to our own needs and inspirations.

We cannot build strong and able corporations until we become strong and able individuals.

Just as a building's foundation must be dug before we can build, so must we prepare our own personal foundations before we can build companies of strength and utility. The most exciting adventure is to see your life as a journey for you and your company.

Whether you are a director, production line worker, CEO, or secretary, by seeking to better yourself you better your company. The metacenter is inclusive, not exclusive. By developing wisdom, you improve your life and the lives of those around you.

As you metacenter, you see that every person has potential. Each person, like you, is a human being on a journey of discovery, not just a journey of income.

To see your colleague as a human being and to respect the humanity within him is engaging. To see your accounts manager, boss, or teammate as a human being, rather than as a role or title, inspires the relationship. The relationship becomes productive and rewarding.

The metacentered way embraces the world of nine to five — including every aspect of corporate life from mailroom to boardroom, factory floor to salesroom.

The metacentered company is seamless, running between the fabric of human values and inspired productivity. Love, creativity, passion, and responsibility share the same origin — the heart.

People like to belong. Human beings respond and function in an environment of understanding, support, sharing, and working with a common purpose. To manage with humanity encourages insight and ability.

In the past, managing with an iron fist ran together with the oppression of all that was feminine. Fear and greed motivated management. It was an age of us against nature, of management against employee.

By working from our metacenter and the metacenter of our team and company, we create with inspiration.

To be metacentered means to work in a way where you encourage understanding between you and those you interact with. Metacentering is not a battle of convincing or proving — metacentering entails explaining and sharing. Metacentering requires dialogue, not debate. Metacentering requires speaking with the intention that the conversation will enrich your path and the path of another.

When we speak through our heart, amazing things happen. We give power to an exchange when we communicate with intention.

Communicating with intention does not mean controlling the conversation. It is one thing to have a structure or focal point; it is another to have an agenda. Discussion is pointless and infertile when based on agendas. It is powerful when we are prepared to break with ideas and concepts — and allow them to evolve naturally through contribution. Talking with intention means speaking with a dedicated heart, not a strategy.

Many of us hear, yet fail to listen.

A metacentered conversation is an adventure. It provides a doorway to seeing life from a new perspective: problems can dissolve, and solutions and opportunities emerge. A genuine conversation has the power to change worlds. Like life, conversation is a dynamically unfolding event. When you see it this way you give it the chance to be something more.

Through metacentered conversation, a true sharing of inspiration, insight, and knowledge takes place.

We can effect real change in our lives and companies if we choose to *listen*. Productivity improves if companies give serious attention to encouraging their people to listen to each other and their customers.

A considerate and attentive team is a responsive and productive team. A metacentered company is a force to be reckoned with, because it responds intelligently to its environment rather than reacting from its own agenda.

Only when you metacenter can your relationships metacenter. The adventure starts with you.

A company dedicated to its success works with its people and cultivates their talents so it can forge new markets, new strategies, new procedures, and new processes. It asks the people in the mailroom how the mail could be managed and delivered more effectively. It asks the people on the factory floor how a car component could be better assembled through revising an assembly process or the design of a part. It asks the people in sales what the customers are looking for, rather than dictating to customers what they can buy.

The metacentered corporation is proactive. It adopts an aggressive approach to ensure that it and its people succeed, while at the same time committing itself to the success of the planet.

Metacenteredness is about aggressive balance in which the needs of you and your company are powerfully met along with the needs of the community and environment.

Many companies have risked and failed. Too many were motivated by the smaller personality of corporate nature —

greed and fear. Their risk was not aligned with heart, but with insecurity. They saw their risk as a financial gamble, not as an opportunity to grow for the benefit of self and world.

Rarely have we seen companies acting from the noble personality of corporate nature — inspiration, vision, commitment, and courage — from which they strive, discovering new markets, contributing to humanity and the earth in meaningful ways.

The more a company invests courage, vision, and commitment in its people, including its suppliers, contractors, and distributors, the more it aligns with success. The more people know they are valued and part of a team, the more they strive to meet deadlines, take initiative, and innovate.

We have not begun to see what a company can do when it is guided by love. To see your company or team as driven by anything less than love is to sever potential and rob you, your family, and the world of a better future.

Relating

One of the key ways to work as a team and negotiate successfully is to realize how diversely others see the world. It is also to value difference and capitalize on it, rather than ignore it and suffer lost profit and conflict because of this ignorance.

Daily, we forget that the way others have experienced the world differs from our own. Our experiences define us: our childhood, our education, our triumphs, our pain — all have shaped us.

Each of us occupies a unique reality: no one else in the world experiences life in the precise way you do. You are unique, and so is the way you see the world. Yet we forget this fact every day of our lives. This can cause bad communication, broken deals, and conflict.

On a cross-cultural level, a new dimension of alternate reality comes into play. As the world becomes a global culture, and as we work and live with people from cultures different from our own, holding an awareness of alternate realities becomes crucial.

Every day we neglect the nuances and priorities of cultures different from our own. We assume that others think and feel in the same way we do. They don't. Feelings, thoughts, needs, and desires span diverse possibilities. In the same way, our languages are worlds apart. So is the way we relate to happiness and conflict, time and space.

Misunderstanding alternative realities in commerce can be disastrous for negotiations, operations, administration, and sales. Knowing your product, market, and competition is vital to survival. To learn and grow from the alternate views of co-workers provides us with more ways to innovate, produce, and sell.

A company's awareness of how other cultures work and how people from other cultures think determines the degree to which it succeeds internationally. Business hinges on people: it is there to supply demand. If we do not understand the people — or their demand — how are we to effectively sell, negotiate, or operate?

The metacentered company is one that works and responds to the challenges of cross-cultural interaction. It does not stride headlong into foreign lands believing its way is the right way and its world is the only world. The metacentered way embraces differences and learns through diversity. The metacentered business achieves success in the world by coming to know it and understand it, not contort it and control it.

To carry respect for alternate realities into a morning meeting or a major international deal can make all the difference between communication and misunderstanding, synergy and breakdown.

Innovation

Innovation is an effect of responsiveness. Rather than react with old strategies, innovation comes when we examine difficulty, assess strengths and weaknesses, and develop a solution by which to overcome the difficulty. The metacentered company responds to challenge — not reacts to it — and navigates its way through unforeseen obstacles.

In the same way that metacentering realigns a person's daily life with his heart's vision, a company's culture, product, and operations can be realigned with the company's vision. What does not serve the purpose and ambition of the company is eliminated and replaced with something of utility and purpose.

The word *innovate* means renew. Innovation is the native tongue of creativity. Your creativity is drawn from an old and powerful place — your imagination. Your imagination draws on a storehouse of millions of years of inherited wisdom.

We are a developing species. Within every one of us lives primal talent and ancient wisdom. To lose touch with it is fatal to realizing potential. Kill your imagination and you kill success.

Innovation is the language of the metacentered.

To be innovative is to effectively respond to challenge and opportunity. It is a way of life, and it is a state of being in which we are inwardly collected, ready for the obstacles and shortcuts that come with unexpected turns in the road.

Businesses inhibit success by applying old solutions to new problems. Like fitting a square block into a round hole, the solution proves ineffective. It is one thing to work with education and the strategies of our predecessors; it is another to be servant to them.

Metacentering requires thinking and acting for ourselves. New terrain demands new strategies. The best strategies of commerce, war, and social change did not fall out of a textbook; they rose from vital minds under the insistence of the moment.

Success is tied up in finding the courage to listen to your intuition and having the wisdom to follow it.

Formal education gives us a bird's-eye view for examining past challenges and evaluating how people dealt with them. Education is not about emulating our predecessors. It is about understanding the subtleties and ways of the world so we can develop our own unique language to address them.

But by presuming that education holds the answers, we inhibit the answers from flowing. Wisdom and resourcefulness suffer when we give undue emphasis to the past.

A strategy to meet rising inflation — for example, by lifting interest rates — may have been useful in the past. Yet in the hurricane of a faster-moving economy, fresh strategies may prove more effective. Like an expert warrior of yesteryear facing an opponent of today, the sword — irrespective of who is wielding it — has negligible value in meeting the onslaught of firearms.

We underestimate what can emerge from within us. By finding the courage to think the new, radical, and even stupid, we innovate. By cultivating the strength to risk, we discover our greater personality and special abilities. We become an asset to our company and the world.

We deprive ourselves when we assess our gifts and abilities according to standard expectations — the measurements of the past — the norm. As economics teaches us, by adhering to the norm, we stagnate. It is in creating the new that we create a new market.

Look at the world of one hundred years ago. Today's world is very different, and we live our lives in very different ways. What would your life be like had people not risked and innovated? If we were to travel back one hundred years to describe today's world, people of a century ago would think us mad — or writers of science fiction.

Like the metacentered person, the metacentered company needs to be braced for change. This means embracing the unknown of an unsure world and fickle market.

As talents and path emerge, you may find your current career or product obsolete, or your career or product not harnessing all that your company or you have to offer. You may find your career or product line not capitalizing on your potential. Passion that may have been aflame in the past may have long since burnt out. For some, that may mean a small adjustment. For others, it could mean something more radical.

Companies should be open to cross-fertilization between departments.

Dissatisfied employees loyal to the company but tired with their role should be encouraged to explore other fields. A capable accountant, lawyer, doctor, or engineer can become a formidable asset in a field entirely unrelated to her original profession. It is how we think that is important — not how we have been taught.

The more a company adheres to the old ways of compartmentalizing a person by education, the more it limits itself. People respond to variety and challenge.

Just as metacentering embraces the potential locked in change, so, too, must a company embrace the reality that its people will desire varied experiences during their careers. Variety is a human necessity; as the old adage says, a change is as good as a holiday. When a company ignores its people's need for change and challenges, it risks losing competent minds and jeopardizes success.

Even if employees require further education, a company can help them incubate their new careers while furnishing them with the space and support to flourish. This does not mean babysitting staff or protecting them. Metacentering is about encouragement and enthusiasm. It centers on giving people the space to thrive and become all they can be.

This positive and sincere in-house attitude can only reap profit and satisfaction.

People respond more effectively to a healthful environment than to an exorbitant salary. Dollars are not enough to motivate us to brilliance. We may hold focus for a time, but when we eventually reach that tempting carrot, we discover it does not taste as we anticipated. We must pursue heart, not just pocket.

Today's company must take responsibility for its destiny, the people that make it, and the world it does business in. It must claim its place in the world, just like the rest of us.

Responding with courage, vision, and a commitment to the human spirit and a healthy profit is the metacentered way to achieve this.

Metacentered World

Twelve

C OMMUNITY IS THE foundation for humanity. The evidence of what we can create by working together is startling: Mozart's compositions were made possible by the instruments and recitalists of his time, Einstein developed his theory of relativity after studying his peer's insights into time and reality, Picasso created cubism after exploring the techniques of other masters, Louis Pasteur discovered vaccines after studying the findings of the scientists before him, Frank Lloyd Wright built the Guggenheim Museum thanks to modern materials and engineering, Gandhi developed his philosophy of non-violence through the insights of philosophers and activists, and Sir Tim Berners-Lee invented the worldwide web, which was given life through you and me.

Through the talent of cooperation, world technology has allowed us to become global. We are no longer solely Christian, Jewish, or Muslim, but members of a global order. However, despite being linked by the infrastructure of our technology, we are not yet linked by our hearts.

Until one hundred years ago, our errors, such as environmental damage and bloodshed, were localized. A war in one faraway country was, at worst, a terrible tale in another. But over the last one hundred years that has changed. The destiny of one place has become intertwined with the destiny of others.

We are no longer solely American, European, or Asian, but citizens of Earth.

Our new global citizenship requires that we try to understand each other's beliefs and dreams and each other's pain and past.

Impact

It is easy amidst global tribulations to lose faith. It is easy to switch on the news, see hurricanes, bloodshed, and plunging economies and decide, "It is too hard to think about the world."

We lose faith because we watch too much television, read too much news, listen to too much radio, and allow this neon reality to become the state of the world. It is easy to understand how so many of us forget our potential. However, if you stop and look around, you discover the world is full of quiet heroes.

We lose sight of the reality that every moment we are alive, we affect the world we live in. Every action and non-action has an impact: from deciding how we dispose of our household waste to showing courtesy on the road, from everyday interactions with our colleagues to a moment's conversation in the street.

Even our thoughts have an effect. Quantum physics tells us there is no separation in the language of the universe: only synchronicity, connectedness, and flow. The very fact of our existence presents us with the creative opportunity to make an impact on the world in which we live.

When we get swallowed by the day, it is easy to forget that we are a part of something magical. Harmony is a discipline. Harmony requires right attitude, self-belief, and adherence to vision. The very challenges that the world presents to us are drivers in our journey to achieve harmony.

Every minute of the day you make a difference. Whether the difference is positive or negative is up to you. How you make an impact on the world is a choice. Your very existence embodies unfathomable creative potential.

One practical example of how you make an impact on the world is the decision of how to dispose of your computer. Unwittingly, when you discard your computer, you may be killing the environment and people's health on the opposite side of earth. Over half the computers in the USA are shipped to China, India, and Pakistan. In Guiyu, China, men, women, and children pull wiring from the terminals and burn them at night, filling the air with toxic smoke. Others work for $1.50 a day, with little or no protection, burning circuit boards and pouring acid on electronics to extract silver and gold. Others pry open printer cartridges and smash cathode ray tubes laden with lead. The groundwater in Guiyu is undrinkable. One water source is one hundred and ninety times the toxicity level allowed by the World Health Organization.

The computers spread across the land still have the names of their owners in America; ordinary people like you and me. Little things, like the way we discard our computers matter. Remember the startling mathematical phenomenon called the Butterfly Effect? It proves that the smallest act can make a formidable impact. Just as the flutter of a butterfly's wings can cause a hurricane, the tiniest action, such as how you decide to discard your computer, can make an impact on the world.

Silent impact

One of the great masters of impact was Mahatma Gandhi. Through his principle of applied truth called satyagraha, Gandhi innovated a way of impact that achieved independence for India. Gandhi was a master of silent impact — he didn't seek to obstruct flow, but to step out of it, and through doing so, he changed it. As a lawyer, he understood the legal and commercial nuances of the British Empire. For example, by leading the Indian people to refuse the salt tax, he brought the Empire to a standstill. The Empire relied on the machinery of the Indian people to keep it operating. By removing the people's willingness to participate, the machine was incapacitated.

Market impact

Whether we know it or not, we have tremendous impact. The number of conscious consumers in the world is growing dramatically, and the conscious consumer market even has a name — Lifestyle of Health and Sustainability (LOHAS). In America, the LOHAS market amounts to fifty million adults, and in the European Union, eighty million. It is a $540 billion global market. With this in mind, how do you think silent impact could work in the world of capitalism?

Example of a solution for whaling

In June 2006 a controversial move toward recommencing commercial whaling occurred as a result of a one-vote difference in the International Whaling Commission.[15]

A friend, David, was visibly upset by the decision and exclaimed "I am so angry." He felt ordinary people were disempowered from making a difference. So I asked him, if Gandhi were alive today, how would he approach it? What could the principle of silent impact achieve? We considered the relevant facts. The move toward recommencing commercial whaling is driven by Japan and rooted in market demand. Japan is a major manufacturer of products worldwide. Many customers located in places such as Australia, New Zealand, Europe, America, and Canada who buy Japanese products object to whaling. We pondered: what would it look like if suddenly conscious customers mobilized around a movement that agreed to buy products only from Japanese companies opposed to whaling and actively showing their opposition? These approved companies could not engage in any commerce with or shareholding in a Japanese company associated with whaling. Sure, it would take some good minds to formulate an approach that could ensure effect and compliance, but thankfully, the world is not short of good minds. There are brilliant people all around us, just waiting to get involved in meaningful projects.

Silent impact within

Silent impact is not just applied to the world, but to ourselves. The principle of silent impact means overcoming ourselves for the betterment of the world. For example, during their fight for independence it took extreme acts of inner strength for the Indian people to resist aggressive retribution toward the Empire — even in the wake of massacres and beatings, the Indian people stayed anchored to outcome through peaceful means at risk of death. Conscious consumers who are coordinated around a cause, such as the elimination of whaling, need to be anchored. They cannot sway from the cause. They must be unwavering in how they apply their power as consumers. Through coordinated strikes of purchasing or non-purchasing, these actions have the power to overturn markets and effect how the businesses of the world operate. The Amazon, which provides twenty percent of the earth's oxygen, is being killed at a rate of 12,800 football fields a day so we can get a hamburger at a fast-food restaurant. The timber used in your house could well have been felled from vast virgin rainforests in Indonesia. Rainforests are being felled there at a rate of 9,580 football fields per day.

The Internet is an initiation into conscious consumerism. You now have the ability to make informed purchases and help redirect how the resources of the world are harvested.

Gandhi knew, just as Christ, the Prophet Mohammed, and the Buddha knew, that every one of us is powerful. We have reservoirs of wisdom and stamina that await a purpose.

Every human being on earth is enabled by the existence of every other human being. A new discovery in biology called morphic resonance has revealed that we are all connected by fields of energy, and our ability to learn and master something is accelerated when another has mastered that act before us. When we coordinate around a cause and develop our skill at being a conscious citizen of Earth, we help all people to coordinate and become conscious. I believe this phenomenon helped the Indian people to master silent impact and coordinate around the cause for their independence, and I believe this phenomenon will help each of us to develop our consciousness and coordinate around the cause for a conscious world.[16]

Cooperation — like success — is a decision. It demands questioning, courage, commitment, and vision. Only you can decide what you want your life to be and what you want your world to become.

Community can become the mantra of this new century. Through community, we transcend differences and achieve solutions.

You can make a difference. You make an impact on this world — from a simple smile at a person in the street, to sharing an idea on the Internet, to consciously discarding your computer, to introducing a social project in your company.

What can you, your family, and company start today? Think beyond yourself and into the world.

The size of the act is irrelevant. It is the quality of heart with which we perform the act that is vital.

Even the simplest act executed with the purest intention can change the world.

Freedom's Way

Vision Drivers:
Nine Tools to Metacenter Your Life

Your ability to communicate
Your life's circumstances
Your dedication
Your ability to question

Your Vision

Part 4

Vision Drivers for Living

Thirteen

NOW YOU ARE ready to apply the principles you have been reading about.

To successfully metacenter, you need these three key elements:

1. Vision
2. Courage
3. Execution

Freedom's Way echoes throughout its pages that your life is a choice. The following guidelines help you choose your path.

We all agree with the need for vision and courage when we read about it. But reading about the value of vision and the need for courage is one thing; implementing them is another, especially when we are confronted by life's everyday challenges: a wounded relationship, a job retrenchment, or something as devastating as being diagnosed with cancer.

Vision and courage relate to our every moment. In fact, when our life's vision dims, the world darkens along with it. We become blind to what lies in front of us and what lies within us.

Your vision for a healthy relationship, a rewarding career, a vital body, and a fulfilling life overall — those visions are your stencils for success.

Whether you are aware of it or not, you *do* have a vision of what you want your world to become, what you want your relationship to become, what you want your company to become — and what you want your life to become. Implementing your vision begins with you.

Every moment counts. Every action and non-action, every communication and every silence, has an effect. Even when you are alone, your decision to turn on the television or to sit quietly, to reflect, think, and commune with your surroundings, to review the day or to plan the next — all these affect your equilibrium and conviction.

Each decision affects your future and the futures of those with whom you share your life's time: from a vague acquaintance at the bus stop to your significant other, child, or co-worker. Every moment counts because it leads into and determines the next moment.

Scope

Success encompasses five major areas:

1. Your vision for life
2. Your vision for relationship

3. Your vision for family

4. Your vision for work

5. Your vision for the world

You can define your vision for each of these five areas by using of a unique tool called a *vision driver.* Four additional drivers are offered in Chapter Fourteen for those who are currently experiencing a crisis.

Each vision driver encompasses of a set of *vision triggers* and a process. Vision triggers are questions designed to trigger a response in you that helps define and shape your vision. The process involves a sequence of five steps through which you develop your own vision. These steps are:

1. Find your vision — ***Envision.***

2. Cultivate the courage to apply your vision — ***Self-encourage.***

3. ***Align*** this vision to your life. This is what it means to metacenter your life.

4. ***Feedback*** — Observe, question, and reflect as alignment starts to reshape your life, relationship, work, world, and family. See how your attempts at alignment can be honed and how your vision can be refined.

5. ***Realign*** — Hone your vision by going back to Step 1.

Life Vision Driver

Suggestions

If the concept of a life vision appears grandiose and hard to get your mind around at first, sit down with a pen and start writing as you read. Before you know it, you will realize that your vision is far more specific and far-reaching than you ever realized.

This is a metacentering exercise and is most effective when done periodically — every few weeks to every few months. In fact, if you are dedicated to your vision, you will eventually use it to hone your success and actualize your dreams moment to moment through your relationships, work, and world.

Every moment counts. The clearer you become, the more successful you are, because you see what is needed to align your reality with your vision and work toward it without the inner resistance of insecurity, fear, and lack of faith.

Suggested reading

If it has been more than a couple of months since you read *Freedom's Way,* review these chapters:

2   Silent Stillness

1   New Beginnings

Vision triggers

What were your dreams as a child?

What feelings are evoked when you pause and revisit any old memorabilia you have, including school-books and photographs, so you can reconnect with that time?

Who did you want to be?

Who were you before life took hold?

What did you want to become as a person?

How does that feel?

Do you feel satisfied with who you are and where you are today in comparison to those memories, or do you feel dissatisfied?

If you were able to put all the commitments, fears, and resistance aside and hold up your childhood vision, would it still be your vision?

What would you have to change to give it new life now?

What fears are evoked?

Where do those fears come from?

If those fears were gone, who would you be?

What are you compelled to become?

What excites you about life and being a part of it?

When you are at the end of your life, how do you want to feel when you look back upon it?

1. *Envision* — Define your vision. How did you feel when reading the vision triggers? What did they inspire? How did they motivate you? Write it down.

2. *Self-encourage* — Cultivate the courage and determination to implement your vision.

3. *Align* the vision to your life.

   a. Align your life vision with your ability to communicate. Have you created a circle of clarity around your life in order to implement your vision? Do you tell others how you feel? Do you acknowledge to yourself how you feel?

Do you think expressing your feelings is a strength or a weakness? If it is a weakness, how do you expect to change things in your life if you hold your silence with those who share your life — your family, your spouse, your colleagues?

Do you sit with yourself? Do you respect your need for space? Have you made room in your life for your life vision? Do you ever feel scared? If not, why not? When you feel scared or stretched, do you stay true to your vision?

b. Align your life vision with your *life's circumstances.* Is your life vision aligned with your work, relationship, family, and the world? If not, what can you do to change it? How big is the gap between your life currently and your vision for it? What can you do to close the gap?

Imagine you are someone else. What are five feasible things you suggest to close the gap and work toward making your vision a reality?

c. Align your life vision with your *dedication.* Are you committed to seeing your vision through? Are you resisting changes necessary to execute your life vision? If so, why?

What could you do to change this? Do you think the resistance is sensible or based on fear and self-doubt? If the resistance stems from self-doubt, are your doubts rational? If your doubts are rational, what can you do to remove them? How hard are you working to remove doubt?

What can you do differently to make your vision a reality? Do you believe that life would start to work with you if you started to believe in yourself? Do you believe in yourself? Be honest; don't let yourself get away without answering. Stop, take a deep breath, and genuinely think about this.

Every one of us has doubts at times — that is why there is a concept called faith. When was the last time you risked? What can you do to believe more in yourself?

d. Align your life vision with your ability to question. Do you question your life and ask how it can be bettered? Are you content with your current life? Is your current life aligned with your vision? If not, are you truly content or have you compromised your happiness because you somehow believe you do not deserve something better? What can you do to change this situation if it applies to you?

Do you ask moment to moment how you can align your friendships, work, relationship, family, and the world with your vision? If not, why not? Would you like your life to reflect your vision? How could this be achieved? What are five things you can do to begin changing this?

4. ***Feedback*** — Observe, question, and reflect to see how your attempts at alignment can be honed and how your vision can be refined.

5. ***Realign*** — Hone your vision by going back to Step 1.

Relationship Vision Driver

Suggestions

Do this exercise individually, then as partners, and journey through it together. This is a metacentering exercise and is most effective when repeated periodically, from every few weeks to every few months.

Suggested reading

If it has been more than a couple of months since you read *Freedom's Way,* review these chapters:

9   Metacentered Relationship
2   Silent Stillness
10   Metacentered Family
6   The Rise of Anger

Vision triggers

⊗   What is your vision as a couple?

What are your needs and dreams as two people on the journey of life together?

What do you want to give?

What do you want to receive?

Who do you want to become as a result of the union with your partner?

1. ***Envision*** — Define your vision for relationship. How did you feel when reading the vision triggers? What did they inspire? How did they motivate you? Write it down.

2. ***Self-encourage*** — Cultivate the courage and determination to implement your vision.

3. ***Align*** the vision to your life.

   a. Align your vision for relationship with *communicating*. Are you staying true to your vision? Do you hold to your togetherness and talk through the trying times, or do you allow reactions to get the better of you?

   What three things could you do to stay responsive during heated times? During heated times, are you asking yourself "am I being metacentered in how I am dealing with this?"

b. Align your vision for relationship with your *life's circumstance.* Is your home aligned with a habitat that supports your relationship? (For example, are you near or far from work, near or far from family? Is your home a place you like to return to? Is it a sanctuary? Does it inspire you? If not, what could you do to change that?)

Is your work aligned with your relationship? Does work inhibit your love for each other or encourage it? Do you want children? If you have children, do you and your partner ensure time for each other amidst the demands of parenthood? You don't serve your child if you neglect each other.

Did you want to explore the world together? Did you want to live in a different city or in the country? Have you become bogged down in circumstances that were never meant to be "a part of the plan"?

c. Align your vision for relationship with *supportiveness.* Do you encourage your partner to align with his or her own life's vision? Are you supportive? Do you listen to your partner?

How often do you communicate (through words or action) how you feel about your partner — that you believe in, are inspired by, and find meaning through your union with your partner?

d. Align your vision for relationship with *understanding, dedication,* and *respect.* When you argue, do you "fall into camps" and allow your argument to become destructive, or do you hold true to your relationship's vision and use differences as a bridge to growth and a better understanding of each other?

Do you see your relationship as a circumstance or as a life purpose? Do you find enrichment from your connection?

Often the answer to these questions is in the negative, not because we fail to love our partners, but because we have allowed less important things to dominate our attention. It is one thing to work hard to pay off the mortgage for that dream home, but it defeats the purpose, does it not, if your love for each other dies in the process? As part of the human condition, we tend to take what we have for granted; like our heart, our husband or wife feeds us with life, yet in the day-to-day we forget how vital our partner is.

4. *Feedback* — Observe, question, and reflect to see how your attempts at alignment can be honed, and how your vision can be refined.

5. *Realign* — Hone your vision by going back to Step **1.**

Family Vision Driver

Suggestions

Do this exercise individually, then sit together as a family and experience it together. This is a metacentering exercise and is most effective when done periodically — from every few weeks to every few months — from a quick review over a family dinner to a family weekend away.

Suggested reading

If it has been more than a couple of months since you read *Freedom's Way,* review these chapters:

10   Metacentered Family
6   The Rise of Anger
2   Silent Stillness

Vision triggers

What do you want as a family?

What do you want to gain?

What do you want to give?

What do you want to achieve together?

What is your idea of a harmonious family?

What would you like your family to be?

How do you think it could be achieved?

Be aware, as you travel through these questions and define your vision, that every family is different. That is what makes family beautiful. Work toward discovering the uniqueness within your family's soul: only then will you discover purpose and power as a family unit.

1. *Envision* — Define your vision as a family. How did you feel when reading the vision triggers? What did they inspire? How did they motivate you? Write it down.

2. *Self-encourage* — Cultivate the courage and determination to implement your vision.

3. *Align* the vision to your life.

    a. Align your vision for your family with *communicating.* Do you listen and share in a way aligned with your vision? Do you speak your heart? When you speak your heart, do you do so out of anger and resentment, or out of the need to bring clarity and love back to your relationship?

b. Align your vision for your family with *under-standing.* Do you see the beauty and diversity of members of your family being able to view life in ways different from your own? Do you see differences as a road to enrichment and greater learning, or as hindrances?

Family is one of the most powerful ways to achieve mastery. When you master communicating with your family and understand them, you will be in a good position to master most life situations.

c. Align your vision for your family with *dedication.* Are you dedicated to seeing your vision through? In the midst of fury, do you stay metacentered and true to your vision, or do you let yourself be swayed by the anger of the moment? It is one thing to work with your anger and stay true to your vision; it is another to allow it to become destructive and jeopardize the vision you have been working toward.

Are you dedicated to seeing your vision becoming a reality in every moment — even the most trying?

d. Align your vision for your family with *respecting.* Do you respect your family's right, even need, to make mistakes? Do you see forgiveness as a duty, or as a necessity to achieve love? Do you accept that not everyone in your family will have a vision for family concomitant with your own?

4. **Feedback** — Observe, question, and reflect to see how your attempts at alignment can be honed and how your vision can be refined.

5. **Realign** — Hone your vision by going back to Step 1.

Company Vision Driver

Suggestions

Do this exercise individually, then sit together as a team, even as a company, and envision it together. This is a metacentering exercise and is most effective when done periodically, from every few weeks to every few months, from a quick review over lunch once the vision is "up," to a few days in duration, preferably with time in between to allow for insight and reflection.

Suggested reading

If it has been more than a couple of months since you read *Freedom's Way,* review these chapters:

- 11 Metacentered Company
- 2 Silent Stillness
- 6 The Rise of Anger

Vision triggers

- What do you want to achieve as a worker? (Every one of us is a worker, whether farming a field, defending someone in court, or heading the United Nations; the key is to quietly ask yourself: Am I happy with what I am working toward?)

- What do you want to achieve as an employee, as a team, and as a company? Be honest; don't let yourself or anyone on your team get away without answering. Stop and genuinely think about this.

- Is happiness important?

  What would you have to change to be happy at work?

  What is it about your work, your company, and your product that is important to you?

  What would you have to change in order to cherish what you do for a living?

- What could be done better to improve product, service, or workplace?

- If there were a notion called "love" at work, how would it operate?

  How would your company look and operate if it were to be an absolute success for people and profit?

1. *Envision* — Define your vision. How did you feel when reading the vision triggers? What did they inspire? How did they motivate you? Write it down.

2. *Self-encourage* — Cultivate the courage and determination to implement it.

3. *Align* the vision to your life.

    a. Align your vision for work with *communicating*. Are you honest? Do you say what you feel? Do you stay true to your vision when you e-mail, telephone, and speak to others? When you have an argument or heated exchange with a colleague, do you hold to the vision or do you allow yourself to get caught up in the anger of the moment?

    Do you listen? Do you acknowledge that things can always be improved? Do you accept that you can be wrong? Do you recognize mistakes as an essential part of achieving success?

    b. Align your vision for work with *questioning*. Do you sit at your desk or stand on the factory floor and just "do the day," or do you look at your computer, tools, customers, and circumstances and continuously ask how you can align your vision to process, people, and product?

Do you observe yourself through the day and ask, "Am I communicating and performing in a way that is consistent with my vision?" Do you ask yourself every day how you can improve product, relationships, and workplace?

c. Align your vision for work with *support.* Do you see every person as a human being first and a role second? Do you encourage your colleagues, customers, and suppliers? Do you encourage others in their journey to stay true to their vision and the vision of the company? Do you see that each individual makes the company or workplace what it is?

Do you accept that someone who is "soft on vision" and fails to actualize it in the workplace affects everyone through profit and personality? Do you accept that attitude is crucial? Do you seek to ensure that your colleagues are happy and aligned with your company's goals?

d. Align your vision for work with *people, operations,* and the *market:*

- *People.* Is the company's vision consistent with its people and their attitudes, roles, and responsibilities? How can it be improved? Are people satisfied with their duties and responsibilities? Are people happy?

Does the company ensure that all participate in making the vision reality? Do all have a say in how things can be improved? Is feedback encouraged so the vision can keep being honed?

Does the company strive or does it exist? What can be done to bring the vision forward? How can the current situation be improved?

- *Operations.* Are all operations consistent with the vision? Is process, whether on the factory floor, in the accounts section, or in customer relations, as aligned with the vision as possible?

How would the people in manufacturing, accounts, or sales improve the current process to make it more effective and "true to vision"? How often is this question asked? Be honest; genuinely think about your answer.

How much money could be made and saved if this question were asked more regularly? Would you say that any section of your operations was metacentered? If not, what would it take to change that?

- *Market.* Is your product the best it can be? If the answer is "yes," read the question again. When was the last time you asked customers if they were happy with the product? When was the last time you asked customers whether they were happy with the service?

  Do you see the customer as your employer and the reason for your business? Do you seek to improve the life of your customers or simply to sell them a product? Are these questions relevant to your vision? If not, why not?

  How can you deepen your vision so you can make it more successful for people and profit?

4. *Feedback* — Observe, question, and reflect to see how your attempts at alignment can be honed, and how your vision can be refined.

5. *Realign* — Hone your vision by going back to Step 1.

World Vision Driver

Suggestions

Your world vision is important. Everything you do has an impact on community. Do this exercise in the same way as you approach your life's vision. This is a metacentering exercise and is most effective when done periodically — every month, every few months, or semiannually.

Suggested reading

If it has been more than a couple of months since you read *Freedom's Way,* review these chapters:

12 Metacentered World
 2 Silent Stillness
 6 The Rise of Anger

Vision triggers

What worries you about the world today?

What inspires you about the world today?

⊛ Do you believe you can make a difference?

If not, why not?

Do you believe humanity is only as successful as the people who make it?

What can you do to contribute?

1. **Envision** — Define your vision. How do you feel when reading the vision triggers? What do they inspire? How do they motivate you? Write it down.

2. **Self-encourage** — Cultivate the courage and determination to implement your vision.

3. **Align** the vision to your life.

   a. Align your vision with *communicating*. When you see someone who looks different from you, your family, or friends, how do you feel? Do you feel scared, angry, or different? Why do you think this is? When you see another person in the street who looks the same as you, do you smile or look down? What if the person looks different? If you look down or away: why? Are these feelings consistent with your world vision? How do you think you can close the gap?

   b. Align your world vision with *cooperation*. Is your vision aligned with the way you interact with others? Do you work at having effective exchanges with people? Do you believe that a smile or a warm word can change another person's day, or, at times, even her or his life? Do you remind yourself daily about the power of love?

c. Align your vision with *respect:* Do you see a human being or a person when you walk to work? Do you seek to bring your world vision forward even in the most unspectacular circumstances, such as when you are standing in the subway?

Does your world vision come forward every time you are in the presence of another human being? Do you judge others? If your answer is no, ask yourself the question again.

If you judge, why? When you judge, do you realize that you limit your power to expand beyond your current understanding of self and the world? Is your vision aligned with judgment or with working toward connection?

When you respect another, you do so as much for yourself as for the other? When you judge, or more damaging still, allow yourself to hate, you kill the love inside you. You jeopardize the peace and power you have worked so hard to cultivate. Think of Mahatma Gandhi's example of silent impact. This extraordinary act of self-control can be a powerful reminder — even a motivator — for you in protecting your attitude when you feel tempted to judge another. It can also help put things back into perspective: if Gandhi and the Indian people could achieve silent impact within, and in so doing achieve independence for India, we can remember our world vision and stay true to it and true to ourselves.

How often in a day do you allow yourself to judge?

d. Align your vision with action. What are you doing to make your world vision a reality? What are three things you could do for your community? What are three things you could do for your wider community, the world?

Is your world vision aligned with your work? If not, what could you do to close the gap? Would it be possible to create a team that could pool skills and apply them to a cause? If properly thought out, such a team would benefit your company *and* the world because the team would receive a sense of satisfaction, and the company would benefit by the team's attaining additional skills, experience, and perhaps new relationships and ideas.

What world vision could create added value for your business?

4. *Feedback* — Observe, question, and reflect to see how your attempts at alignment can be honed, and how your vision can be refined.

5. *Realign* — Hone your vision by going back to Step 1.

Vision Drivers for Crisis

Fourteen

The following vision drivers can help you or those around you face some of life's hardest ordeals.

Four drivers are offered for:

⊛ working with a life-threatening illness,

⊛ dealing with tragedy,

⊛ experiencing divorce, and

⊛ healing a wounded relationship.

Using these drivers can help you manage the pain and convert an awful situation into one of meaning and enrichment.

These drivers can help you rise above the intense insecurity you may be feeling, and transform the energy you may be expending in fear into new understandings and replenishment.

Illness

Suggestions

This is a metacentering exercise and is most effective when done periodically — daily, every few days, or every few weeks. It can also be used by those who are not working with an illness, but simply want to remember what is important in their lives. It is a powerful exercise for every one of us.

Suggested reading

If it has been more than a couple of months since you read *Freedom's Way,* review these chapters:

7 Suffering
4 Surrender
2 Silent Stillness
6 The Rise of Anger

Vision triggers

Before reading further, take a deep breath and rest into yourself.

⊛ Do you believe it is okay to feel scared?

Do you listen to your heart, your dreams, your fears, your innocence?

Do you believe your heart is a source of strength or weakness?

Do you believe that new life and understanding could come from your illness?

Do you believe opportunity might be hidden in even the most awful of circumstances? If not, try to reflect on whether this attitude is conducive to your healing.

Do you think about death?

What do you think about it?

Do you seek to understand it?

Does it scare you?

How much does it scare you?

Do you think there is potential in coming to understand those fears and resolving them rather than shutting them out or trying to will them away?

⊛ Do you believe that we teach and learn from each other?

Do you believe that the way you live with your illness can have a positive effect on others?

⊛ Do you think your illness could be the chance to improve your life: to respect your body, deal with your stress, look at your attitude, and remember the beauty of life?

⊛ How much thought have you put into the prospect that you might die?

Have you been resisting thoughts around your mortality?

How do you think your state of mind and attitude may change if you approach your illness proactively?

⊛ Do you think the way we view death in the modern world is healthy?

Are you trying to heal to avoid death or to seize life?

1. ***Envision*** — Define your vision. How do you feel when reading the vision triggers? Do they inspire you? How do they motivate you? Write it down.

2. ***Self-encourage*** — Cultivate the courage and determination to implement your vision.

3. ***Align*** the vision to your life.

   a. Align your vision about working with this illness with *communicating.* Do you create a circle of clarity around you and give emphasis to your vision? Do your needs come first or after those of others?

   Because healing demands that you focus within and dedicate yourself to your well-being, your first responsibility is to yourself; thus, do you communicate to others how you feel? Do you acknowledge to yourself how you feel? Do you believe that others can learn from your ordeal?

   b. Align your vision about your illness to *dedication.* How dedicated are you to your vision? Do you live your vision every moment? Do you watch your thoughts and feelings? How focused are you on ensuring that your life is aligned to your vision?

   What could you do to enhance your focus? Write down 21 reasonable ideas, choose seven, and apply one per day for three weeks. (If you choose to do this exercise and find it helpful, realign in three weeks and repeat.)

c. Align your vision for working with this illness to your *life's circumstance:* Do you ensure that every aspect of your life's circumstance is aligned with your vision?

If you believe that diet is important, do you eat and drink in a way that is aligned with your vision? If you believe that exercise is important, do you have a routine that is aligned with your vision?

If you believe that attitude is important, do you work at cultivating an attitude aligned with your vision? If you believe that a healthy home environment is important, do you work at ensuring a home environment that is aligned with your vision?

d. Align your vision for working with this illness with your *inner state.* Do you believe attitude makes a difference? If you do, do you ensure that your attitude is aligned moment to moment with your vision? If not, what can you do to change that?

Do you see this illness as a curse of life or as an "initiation" to seeing and understanding life on a deeper level and being better able to help others as a result of that initiation? Are you inwardly dedicated to seeing your vision through? Are you living your vision in your heart?

4. **Feedback** — Observe, question, and reflect to see how your attempts at alignment can be honed, and how your vision can be refined.

5. **Realign** — Hone your vision by going back to Step 1.

Tragedy

Suggestions

This driver is for those who are suffering the loss of a loved one or are affected by global tragedy — something which, by the enormity of the horror, affects your heart and humanity, irrespective of where you live in the world. This metacentering exercise is most effective if done initially every couple of days for a month, then monthly for a year.

Suggested reading

If it has been more than a couple of months since you read *Freedom's Way,* review these chapters:

4   Surrender
7   Suffering
2   Silent Stillness
6   The Rise of Anger
12   Metacentered World

Vision triggers

Take a deep breath and don't hold back your feelings. Let your emotions speak: feel the tears or the anger. Feel the pain; don't try to shut it out or brave the storm with a stoic attitude. You are human. Allow yourself to feel.

⊛ How do you feel?

What is going to change in your life as a result of this tragedy?

⊛ If you have suffered personal loss, how would the person you have lost want you to move forward?

What did you learn from that person? Write down this teaching and attach it to the vision you are creating.

How could you best respect the person's memory while living your future?

What part of that memory gives you purpose?

How could you live your life in a way that incorporates your future with the person's spirit?

⊛ If the tragedy is more far-reaching, such as an event that doesn't directly touch your life but is so tragic that it deeply affects your humanity — how do you feel?

What does this event mean for you?

How can you live in a way that incorporates the memory of the event?

How can you live in a way that gives powerful emphasis — rather than a destructive emphasis — to the memory of those lost?

⊛ Which is more powerful — hate or love?

Recall the Indian people's example of silent impact; how can you best approach a tragic event in a way that inspires your sense of balance, power, and humanity without eroding it?

⊛ How can you live in a way that brings emphasis and respect to the memories of those who were lost?

How can you respond to the tragedy rather than react to it, both within your heart and within your life?

How can you learn by it rather than be dominated by it?

1. ***Envision*** — Define your vision. How do you feel when reading the vision triggers? Do they inspire you? How do they motivate you? Write it down.

2. ***Self-encourage*** — Cultivate the courage and determination to implement your vision.

3. **_Align_** the vision to your life.

   a. Align your vision for working with tragedy with _communicating:_ How do you feel as a result of the loss? Do you allow yourself to feel? Do you tell others how you feel? Do you communicate in a way that is concomitant with your vision? If not, what are three things you could do to change this?

   Do you believe others can learn from you, and vice versa, if you express your feelings? Do you believe others can learn by the way you deal with crisis? If so, would those beliefs help to honor the memory or memories of those who have died? How can you best honor their memory?

   b. Align your vision for working with tragedy with your _life's circumstance._ Is your life aligned with your vision? If not, what could you change? Are you seeking to incorporate the teaching into your life? How do you think this could be done?

   What could you do differently? What could you do more of?

   c. Align your vision for working with tragedy with your _dedication._ Are you dedicated to your vision, to the memory of those lost, and to the teaching, or are you dedicated to the pain of loss?

If you are still held by the pain: what are three things you can do to change your relationship to pain and grow from it? What are three things you can do to change your relationship to pain and grow from it? When you feel pain, do you seek to have a relationship with it and understand it, or do you react to it by shutting it out, drinking, or working excessively? What could you do to change this?

Do you think you could heal the pain in yourself if you sought to understand it? What are you doing to understand your pain: silently stilling, reading supportive material, speaking to someone supportive and helpful?

d. Align your vision for working through tragedy with your *attitude.* How do you feel about your loss? How could you learn from it? How could you carry this "teaching" into your life? Is your vision aligned to this teaching?

The lesson of loss is a terribly hard one. You must ensure that you don't try to smother the lesson with a superficial vision to shut out the pain. Allow your heart and mind to work together. Then you will have a vision of worth and tremendous durability that can change your life for the better.

Is your attitude aligned with your heart and the teaching? Is your vision in accord with the teaching? What can you do to ensure that your teaching is applied to your life? Is your life in accord with the teaching? Write down three things that you can do to close the gap.

4. **Feedback** — Observe, question, and reflect to see how your attempts at alignment can be honed, and how your vision can be refined.

5. **Realign** — Hone your vision by going back to Step **1**.

Divorce

Suggestions

Breaking up is rarely easy. We projected our futures, hopes, and fears on to the one we loved, and we shared our lives with that person — and may still be in love. But it is one thing to love a person; it is another thing to share a life together.

Now that you find yourself on the other side of the relationship, you must be sure about how you want to move forward. You must be strong and hold to your life's vision and to your vision for a new future without that relationship.

It is advisable to reassess your life's vision before working through this vision driver.

We all know that breaking up is difficult. However, be strong and don't slide back into forgetting why you separated or broke up in the first place. And if you feel that after some distance you can give it another try, be sure that this decision is consistent with your vision and that you are being centered in your decision to return.

Reread Chapter Nine, Metacentered Relationship. Then, if you still think the relationship is retrievable, go to the vision driver after this one: Wounded Relationship.

Suggested reading

If it has been more than a couple of months since you read *Freedom's Way,* review these chapters:

2   Silent Stillness

4   Surrender

6   The Rise of Anger

5   Providence

10 Metacentered Family

9   Metacentered Relationship

Vision triggers

How do you feel as a result of the break-up?

What sadness do you have?

What were your hopes?

Shut your eyes for a moment and take yourself back to a real day in the life of your relationship. Were you happy?

Connect with that feeling and give it a name. Every time you feel insecurity or a longing for your old partner, recall that name to remind yourself of the reality of the relationship rather than the fantasy you may bring to it now that you are alone without your companion.

⊛ What do you want your life to be?

Why did you break up?

What was it you didn't receive that you wanted — trust, more intimacy, more support, more tenderness, more laughter?

How did the relationship have an impact on your life? Did it make you feel free or constrained? Be honest; don't avoid answering. Stop, take a deep breath, and genuinely think about this. Were you able to be vulnerable and share your heart? Were caring and support a part of the culture of your relationship?

Go back to that day in real life and remember how you felt. What did you want to do yet felt blocked from doing — see friends, travel, go out, try a new career, move to a new city, rediscover yourself?

⊛ What good things did you gain from the relationship?

What did you learn?

How could you take these lessons into the next part of your life?

1. *Envision* — Define your vision. How do you feel when reading the vision triggers? Do they inspire you? How do they motivate you? Write it down.

2. ***Self-encourage*** — Cultivate the courage and determination to implement your vision.

3. ***Align*** the vision to your life.

    a. Align your vision for a life after break-up with *communicating.* Are you honest with yourself? Are you seeking to implement your vision, or are you sliding back into old patterns? Do you speak to your old partner? If so, do you do so out of insecurity or strength?

    Are you being true to yourself and to your vision or are you being true to your insecurity? What can you do to actualize your vision?

    b. Align your vision for a life after the break-up with your *dedication.* Are you dedicated to creating your vision, or are you sliding back on insecurity? Are you dedicated to yourself or dedicated to your fear that you are not worthy of someone who may be more compatible?

    Do you believe that you are good enough? Do you know what it means to feel free? Have you tested your vision — have you tried living it?

    c. Align your vision for a life after the break-up with your life's *circumstances.* Do you still have your partner's photo on your desk or bedside table? Do you still make love to him or her? Do you still live in a way consistent with the old relationship?

Are you being true to your vision or surrendering to insecurity? If you were fearless, how would you do things differently? How do you think you could move toward that position of strength? What is stopping you? Why? What could you do to change that?

d. Align your vision for a life after break-up with your *attitude.* What could you do to ensure that your vision is aligned with your attitude? Do you believe you have a beautiful life ahead of you without your old partner? If not, why not? Did you believe you had a beautiful life ahead of you when you were with your old partner? Are you being rational?

What can you do to ensure that your attitude stays solid instead of letting it sway toward insecurity and feelings of low self-worth? If you are feeling insecure, do you think that is a good reason to return to your old relationship?

4. **Feedback** — Observe, question, and reflect to see how your attempts at alignment can be honed, and how your vision can be refined.

5. **Realign** — Hone your vision by going back to Step 1.

Wounded Relationship

Suggestions

This vision driver is presented to help you metacenter a relationship in crisis. One of the greatest aids to healing is to acknowledge the need for healing. Use this vision driver after you review your life vision. Bear in mind that you may benefit by also seeking the assistance of a counselor to support you through this process.

Before you begin this exercise, sit alone, quietly; take a deep breath; and look into your heart. Ask yourself: Am I sure I want to heal my relationship? Am I willing to do the hard work to rebuild this partnership and make it an enduring and loving one? Is it worth it? Am I being driven to heal this relationship because of the love I have for my partner, or out of the fear of being alone?

If you are satisfied with your decision, read on.

This is a metacentering exercise and should first be done individually and then together with your partner. Make it a special act that both of you can look forward to. Do this exercise either every three days or weekly for three months, then reduce the exercise to every two weeks or monthly for six months. Then return to the vision driver for Relationship.

Suggested reading

If it has been more than a couple of months since you read *Freedom's Way*, review these chapters:

9   Metacentered Relationship
6   The Rise of Anger
2   Silent Stillness

Vision triggers

Take a deep breath. Shut your eyes. Take yourself back to the force — the love — that brought you together.

⊛ What was it that made your partner different from everyone else?

What drew you to your partner?

⊛ Through the passion of your togetherness — what was it that made you want to build a relationship with that person?

How did you want to build that relationship? What aspects about the person did you want to discover — did you want to travel? Live overseas? Live in another state? Did you want to take on the world together?

What have you done to live out your vision?

How wide is the gap between that original vision and your current life together?

What could you do to close the gap?

How could you change your current lifestyle to make room for this vision?

How could you change your attitudes to allow this vision to become reality? What has been stopping you? Why? Is it your partner or your fears, your unique past and the hurt that came along with it? Are you committed to fighting for this vision? Are you committed to love?

1. ***Envision*** — How did you feel when reading these vision triggers? Did they inspire you? How did they motivate you? Define a renewed vision for your relationship that can accommodate the old dreams but help you work through current resistances. Write it down.

2. ***Self-encourage*** — Cultivate the courage and determination to implement your vision.

3. ***Align*** the vision to your life.

a. Align your renewed vision for relationship with communicating. How do you speak to your partner? Do you listen? Ask yourself the previous question again. What do you do to communicate your love, faith, and support for your partner? How often do you do this: five times a day? Two times a day? Once a week? Once a month?

How often do you forget that your partner is a human being with a heart — with sensitivities — with vulnerabilities — with yearnings? How often do you cultivate the humanity in your partner? How aligned is your vision with your responses to the above? What can you do to change that? Write five of those ideas down, attach these ideas to your answers to the vision triggers, and review them both every morning. If this seems tiring, seriously review your decision to continue the relationship.

b. Align your renewed vision for relationship with your *dedication:* How dedicated are you to seeing your vision through? Why? Write these factors down. Are you satisfied with your responses? Do you believe that loving requires courage and commitment?

How committed are you to seeing your vision through? Close your eyes. Take a deep breath. Picture yourself as old and wonderfully married to your partner. From that vantage point, take a look "back" over the years as you process this vision driver and continue all the way forward to your "old age" picture. What key factor healed your relationship? What did you change or do differently that kept you happy together?

How did you move forward — together? Give the answer to that question a name — like "secret in-gredient X" — or name it after something potent and relevant to you. (Because you are doing this vision driver together after having done it individually, compare your answers and work together toward a joint answer; then, jointly create a third name for how you moved forward together. Recall this third name together every morning before you get out of bed.)

Every time your dedication wanes, recall that name and the feelings associated with it. How aligned is your renewed vision to the answers you are giving to the above? Is there a gap? What can you do to close it?

c. Align your renewed vision for relationship with your *life's circumstances:* What have you done to draw your life's circumstances closer to your renewed vision for your relationship? How much time do you allow for talking and "resting" into each other? Do you treat making love as sex or as communication? When did you last have a holiday together? What did you do last weekend? Was it aligned with your renewed vision? If it was not, why not? What can you do to change this?

How much television do you watch together? Is it conducive to feeling good together and discovering each other? What could you do instead: walk — take a course — learn a sport — watch the stars and share your dreams and insights of the day — refine your visions — plan a dream — cook up a storm — light a candle and make love?

How aligned is your work to your vision for a beautiful relationship? How can you change this? Are you as effective at work as you could be? Do you spend your time through the day constructively or do you work ineffectively, which means remaining at the office until 8 pm? Do you believe a healthy and vibrant relationship would enhance your performance at work? What could you do at work more effectively to realize your renewed vision for a wonderful relationship?

How constructive are you with your children's habits? Do you allow them to control your life and relationship or is there a balance? Do they have a steady sleeping pattern? Do you respect your children — and vice versa? Have you ever explained to your children that Mom and Dad need time together just as they need time with their friends and time to play? Your children are observing you every moment; because you are a large part of their reality, part of their behavior is a result of your relationship's balance or imbalance.

d. Align your renewed vision for relationship with your ability to *question:* Do you get angry? If not, why not? Are you satisfied with your answer to the previous question? How do you work with your anger? Do you observe it, learn from it, and rectify what is causing you pain, or do you lock it in?

Is your anger productive or destructive? What can you do to change this? Write down the three most important insights and review them every three days. Do you observe and question your actions, reactions, and responses? If not, why not? If you do, how closely do you observe them? Be honest; don't let yourself get away without answering. Pause, take a deep breath, and genuinely think about this.

What can you do to improve your ability to question yourself and your life's circumstances to ensure that you are living in a way aligned with your renewed vision for a healthy relationship?

4. **Feedback** — Observe, question, and reflect to see how your attempts at alignment can be honed, and how your vision can be refined.

5. **Realign** — Hone your vision by going back to Step 1.

Where to Now?

O NE OF THE hardest challenges to achieve a metacentered life is to stay committed to the life you feel inspired to live. To help you meet this challenge I created a suite of web tools.

Experience the *meta-analysis*™ and *vision driver*™ at freedomsway.co.uk. These tools offer insight into hidden areas of your life, which until now have been a mystery. Through a step-by-step process I help you identify your current level of metacenteredness and help you to improve your ability to achieve long- and short-term goals. To ensure that you get the most out of your online experience, I give you an explanation in animation, numbers, and words — so regardless of the form of feedback that your mind uses most effectively, you get the information you need to grow. Plus I track your development so you can see your progress every time you get your online report.

For Companies I created a web tool called *Freedom's Way Holographic.* Freedom's Way Holographic enables you to measure the potential of your team or company through each of the people who make it. The results provide you with unique insight into the very core of your organization and help you to identify areas for growth.

See you online!

Endnotes

1. *Bhagavad Gita* (Song of God), Chapter 2, The Yoga of Knowledge.

2. W. J. Cromie, "Meditation Found to Increase Brain Size," *Harvard University Gazette,* 23 January 2006.

3. Daniel Goleman, narrator, *Destructive Emotions and How We Can Overcome Them: A Dialogue with the Dalai Lama,* London: Bloomsbury Publishing, 2003, pp. 179-204.

4. Heinz-Otto Peitgen, Harmut Jürgens, Dietmar Saupe, *Chaos and Fractals: New Frontiers of Science,* 1992, Springer Verlag, New York, p. 355, quoting D'Arcy Thompson, *On Growth and Form,* Cambridge University Press, 1942.

5. Viktor E. Frankl, *Man's Search for Meaning,* transl. Ilse Lasch, New York: Simon and Schuster, 1963, pp. 65–66.

6. The details and quotations have been taken from the film *Lorenzo's Oil,* MCA/Universal City Studios, 1992, and from www.myelin.org and www.stopald.org.

7. For an excellent analysis, read Carl Jung, *Synchronicity: An Acausal Connecting Principle,* Vol 8, Collected Works,

The Structure and Dynamics of the Psyche, 2nd ed., Routledge, 1969, p. 417.

8. Daisetz Suzuki, *Essays in Zen Buddhism* (First Series), Rider and Co., 1949; reissued New York: Grove Press, p. 236.

9. *The Gospel of Thomas: The Hidden Sayings of Jesus,* saying 3, transl. Marvin Meyer, New York: Harper Collins, 1992.

10. *Holy Bible,* John 14:1.

11. *The Upanishads: Breath of the Eternal,* transl. Swami Prabhavananda and Frederick Manchester, Hollywood, CA: Vedanta Press, 1947, p. 210.

12. The swastika is a primal symbol that has been used since ancient times by cultures spanning the globe. For instance, it is a major symbol in the mythologies of Britain, Greece, Scandinavia, Tibet, India, and North America.

13. Joseph Campbell, *The Masks of God, Vol 4: Creative Mythology,* New York: Viking Penguin, 1968, Arkana edition, 1991, pp. 538–40.

14. *Holy Bible,* Proverbs 29:18.

15. This move was embodied in a declaration called the St. Kitts and Nevis Declaration. The main bone of contention was the Japanese proposal to "normalize" the International Whaling Commission (IWC). This aims to take the IWC back to its "original purpose" which, according to Japan, is to manage commercial whaling as it did in 1946. The declaration questions the scientific rationale for the global ban on whale hunting in 1986 and attacks non-

governmental organizations. It lends legitimacy to the scientifically invalid claim that whale populations are responsible for the decline in the world's fisheries. Norway and Iceland are also nations engaged in whaling. For further information see: http://www.iwcoffice.org/_documents/commission/IWC58docs/Resolution2006-1.pdf and http://panda.org/about_wwf/what_we_do/species/our_solutions/policy/iwc/index.cfm?uNewsID=73160

16. Rupert Sheldrake, *A New Science of Life,* Rochester, VT: Park Street Press; March 1, 1995 and Rupert Sheldrake, *The Presence of the Past, Morphic Resonance and the Habits of Nature,* Park Street Press; March 1, 1995.

A Reader's Journey

Gillian, Hurricane Katrina, and a Chance Encounter

MANY PEOPLE SEARCHING for a place in the world refer to a book that gave them strength or that they found strength in. *Freedom's Way* differs from the other titles it may be shelved with at a bookstore or library because instead of telling the reader which path to follow, it empowers the reader to find his or her own path. This was the case for me.

I found *Freedom's Way* after a long and devastating trip home to Louisiana during the weeks following Hurricane Katrina.

In truth, I was at a point in my life where I had to make decisions that I now know were essential to the health and well-being of my entire family.

My family was spread across the southern states (having evacuated at different times) and communication was minimal. When the levees in and around New Orleans broke I knew the homes of everyone who lived near my parents and sisters were gone.

To give a sense of how bad the devastation was from the flooding, it is now almost a year later, yet none of my relatives are living in their homes. Some are living in a trailer parked in their driveway while they work to rebuild. Others are living together in Baton Rouge (45 miles west of the city) because separate, affordable housing simply doesn't exist. These are the lucky ones.

As a doctoral candidate, I had no savings, but I knew I had to get to my family. With the help of a few friends, I was able to fly to Atlanta and then on to Baton Rouge with enough clothing and supplies for those of my family who had made it to those locations.

I was writing my doctoral dissertation when I made the decision to just go, with no knowledge of how bad the situation really was, how I was going to get back, or even how difficult it would be for loved ones to reach me once I was there. I just knew I had to go and use any resources I could find to help my family and others like them. I was able to help in some amazing ways, and would do it again in a heartbeat if needed.

I was unable to return to Boston for several weeks due to lack of a commercial airport in New Orleans. So I faced dissent from many who were worried about my safety, my health, and — believe it or not — my dissertation.

I know all this sounds very negative, and truth is, the hurricane, its destruction, and the remaining consequences of poorly managed reconstruction efforts are bleak. Yet, every day, people get up and make the decision to keep trying, and so do I.

When I returned to Boston, I slept for several days. I felt in some ways as if everything I had was drained out of me, as if I were a hollow shell of me — spiritually, physically, and emotionally. Then I remembered my interaction with Zeph on my flight to Atlanta. Zephyr has a genuine glow around him (really!), so I knew he was someone I could trust. I remember my brother-in-law being so surprised on learning that Zeph had gone out of his way to retrieve a luggage cart for me. He was concerned about Zeph's motives — as if we as humans cannot help another or accept help from another without expectation! Zephyr reminded me that we can work together to help each other find our way in this world, and it is no surprise that *Freedom's Way* reinforced this positive energy with wisdom from the sages and from Zeph himself.

After I returned home as that hollow shell I speak of, I purchased *Freedom's Way*. I read it at night before bed and many afternoons when I was not sure in which direction my life needed to go. *Freedom's Way* helped me find what I knew I had inside of me, but had somehow lost sight of — my vision. As I read chapter after chapter, I felt very connected to my purpose and to other like-minded individuals. I knew that I had to complete my doctoral work and pursue my vision, which I believe differs from the traditional career path of academia. I also feel that one of the messages of *Freedom's Way* is to follow your vision, your dream, and you will find both success (which differs from traditional thought regarding money) and the ability we have to live in a way that meets one's needs while supporting others (either close by or in a global sense) — meeting those needs through collaborative and passionate work.

Now that I can see the end of the writing phase of my work, I feel the future holds opportunities for me that I likely would not have been open to before I read *Freedom's Way* and used its Vision Drivers. *Freedom's Way* is both a pleasure read and a ready reference for anyone who wants to find their way or reexamine the path they have taken.

Ironically, if Hurricane Katrina had not occurred, I might never have met Zephyr and thus may not have been introduced to the brilliant writing of *Freedom's Way*. Things really do happen for a reason.

Dr. Gillian Addison
Boston
July 6, 2006

About the Author

ZEPHYR BLOCH-JORGENSEN inspires people to realize their potential through a revolutionary system called metacentering, a fusion of eternal principles applied to daily life. Zephyr holds two degrees in law, including a Master of Laws in cross-cultural understanding.

The media in India has predicted that he will be "one of the most brilliant minds of this century."—The Asian Age

Zephyr founded freedomsway.co.uk to pioneer the development of an interactive online experience that helps people, families, and companies apply eternal principles to daily life.

Printed in the United Kingdom
by Lightning Source UK Ltd.
133530UK00001B/31-63/A